Catching Them At It!

Catching Them At It!

Assessment in the early years

Sally Featherstone

'**Observation**
Reaching an understanding of children's learning by watching, listening to, and interacting with children as they engage in activities and experiences and demonstrate their specific knowledge, skills and understanding.

Assessment
Involves analysing and reviewing what is known about each child's learning and development to reach informed decisions about the child's level of attainment.'

Early Years Foundation Stage Profile Handbook 2013, (Standards and Testing Agency, DFE, England, 2012)

FEATHERSTONE
AN IMPRINT OF BLOOMSBURY
LONDON NEW DELHI NEW YORK SYDNEY

Published 2013 by Featherstone, an imprint of Bloomsbury Publishing plc
50 Bedford Square, London, WC1B 3DP

www.bloomsbury.com

ISBN 978-1-472-90474-4

A CIP record for this publication is available from the British Library.

Typeset by Fakenham Prepress Solutions, Fakenham, Norfolk NR21 8NN
Printed and bound in Great Britain by CPI Group (UK) Ltd, Croydon CR0 4YY

10 9 8 7 6 5 4 3 2 1

This book is produced using paper that is made from wood grown in
managed, sustainable forests. It is natural, renewable and recyclable.
The logging and manufacturing processes conform to the environmental
regulations of the country of origin.

To see our full range of titles visit www.bloomsbury.com

Contents

Preface: A brief history of assessment

In my long life in early years education, I have been fortunate to experience many developments, fashions, theories, methods and guidance on assessment of learning and attainment. In their time each was a professional, well-meaning attempt to find out and record what children were learning. Some of the initiatives were successful and helpful in the work of practitioners, some were certainly not; some were time consuming, some took almost no time; and of course, some were useful, some were not.

My experience as practitioner, consultant and trainer, although mainly in England, has taken me to many other countries in the UK and elsewhere, and I hope this short introductory journey through previous methods will make sense across the globe, wherever young children are cared for and educated outside their homes.

Previous assessment methods

In the past, there was no real agreement on the best way to assess children's progress and attainment, particularly in the earliest years of childhood. In fact, many practitioners felt that assessment should not be part of their job. Children under five were considered by some to be too young for accurate judgements to be made, and that assessment might 'label' or disadvantage children. Many practitioners thought that their job was to care for children, keep them safe, sociable, clean and tidy, and allow them to play. Of course, these aspects of a practitioner's work are still at the centre of practice, but in many settings assessment is still an emerging art, and many professionals still feel that assessment of very young children is a dark and dangerous art, open to all sorts of abuse and misinterpretation – and we all know situations where this might be the case!

However, in the past those practitioners who were fascinated by children's development, or who wanted to see whether early years provision was making a difference, used all sorts of assessment measures, and I describe some of them here. Some methods were fashionable simultaneously in different settings, and some are still used as part of the 'assessment toolbox', but they have one thing in common

– their use preceded any agreement on what children should be doing and learning, so they were only of use to the practitioners in the setting, and were rarely shared with parents or the children themselves.

The Milestones model

In the days when nursery provision was more about care and less about learning, sets of developmental milestones were devised (often in consultation with the medical profession) and published to help parents and childcare workers to check whether children were growing and developing normally. They were based on average growth and weight statistics, and they listed the things babies and young children were expected to do at different ages, from birth to around five, when children started school. Teachers and nursery nurses adopted and used these developmental checklists to assess children's progress in day nurseries and nursery schools.

The problems

These checklists don't give much leeway for individuals or for the range of normal growth across a group of children, and like all checklists, they are usually closed statements with yes/no answers. The simple nature of the assessment can lead to unnecessary concern about individual children, particularly in parents. The milestones also focused almost entirely on physical and language development, giving a very narrow view of individual babies and children.

What this method looks like now

Milestones checklists are still popular and readily available through the Internet where practitioners and parents can access and use them to assess the progress of babies and children. However, their use in isolation in daycare has decreased as governments have become more interested in the educational advantages of early education, and incorporated the milestones into assessment schedules.

Of course all early years practitioners need to know about child development, and what is generally considered to be the normal path of development for babies and young children. The Early Years Foundation Stage (EYFS) Development Matters Statements in England have given a new look to 'milestones' statements by setting them out in overlapping stages to give a more gentle progression with more space for individual differences in development. They have also been broadened beyond easily observable features to include social, emotional, creative and other aspects of development and learning.

This model is increasingly common across all developed countries where early years education has been recognised as an important stage in its own right.

The 'Catch it if you see it, and wait for the end of primary school' model

In this method teachers collected random information about children when they saw it, often keeping this information in their heads until they completed annual reports or talked to parents and colleagues. At the time, when there were no national expectations in the form of curriculum statements, there was no written description of the desired outcomes of the education system. Teachers did the best they could in assessing children by chance in the early years.

Some nursery classes and schools constructed checklists of expectations, often based on the milestones model. Written records were not universal, and written reports to parents were rare for children in the early years. Children with additional needs were not usually referred, tested or diagnosed by a psychologist until they were seven years old.

The only national tests were at the end of primary education, when a written test of English, mathematics and general knowledge, was taken by all children to establish their attainment. About ten per cent of children passed the 11+ (or its equivalent) and went to selective or grammar schools, the rest failed and went to secondary schools. The central purpose of this test was to identify the children most able to pass this sort of test who, it was therefore deemed would benefit from selective secondary school education.

Some local authorities in England, and Northern Ireland, have retained this test, and offer grammar school education to children who pass the tests. Around 97% of children in the UK now attend comprehensive schools, and do not sit a national test at 11+. This change, and the implementation of national curriculum statements and annual assessments in all countries in the UK, has resulted in a focus on assessment during primary education, so it is no longer possible to leave all assessment to chance or the end of the last year!

The problems

Although this very informal method took very little time to implement, it was possible to get by without collecting any information at all about some individuals or some aspects of development. There was little written or formal curriculum planning, and the practical nature of the early years curriculum meant that there was no marking or grading. The information gathered about individual children remained in the heads of their teachers and was often affected by the random nature of all informal collection.

What this method looks like now

There are still some early years practitioners who think that the 'Catch it if you see it' model is the best one, and are reluctant to adopt a more systematic collection of assessment evidence through observation, particularly because it is more time consuming. All early years frameworks for learning include guidance on assessment, and the latest versions in the UK all emphasise observational assessment, encouraging practitioners to keep paperwork to a minimum, but emphasising the importance of systematic observation across all areas.

The 'If it moves, write about it' model

In this model, teachers and other adults working in the early years wrote lengthy and lovingly crafted 'stories' about each child. These were descriptive accounts of the child and long observations of activities, which were filed in huge ring binders. These were seldom re-read or evaluated and rarely influenced what was planned next. The stories were written during the year and were sometimes summed up in an even longer discursive prose statement at the end of the year.

A few nurseries and schools made a short version of the stories for the next teacher, and in these cases the original work was discarded. In others, the whole huge volume was transferred and often it was never read. Only in the most exceptional settings did parents and the children themselves ever know about their own learning stories, and practitioners seldom used them for planning next steps in learning.

The problems

Records of this sort were extremely time consuming, seen as a real chore, and were such a waste of time, because the information collected was rarely used to change anything. The stories were given to the next teacher who often received several fat files of handwritten stories which they had no time to read, so they often ignored the files and just started where they always did with a new class.

What this method looks like now

Of course, long observations of individual children are still a very valid way of finding out what they know and can do. But now practitioners realise that the observations are of little use unless adults respond to the information they have collected. We also know that the information handed on to the next practitioner or teacher must be both manageable *and* useful, and that huge volumes of unsorted information are usually disregarded.

The 'Let's knit one ourselves' model

This model evolved where teachers and their assistants (who were often nursery nurses), unable to find a model that exactly suited the needs of the children, constructed schedules for assessment themselves, calling these personal profiles or records. The schedules were carefully put together to help adults, and sometimes parents, to understand how well individual children were doing. Groups of teachers and other practitioners tried to systematically cover all aspects of children's learning, and these schedules were an attempt to make children's records more robust and systematic. Most were completed once a term, with a final judgement made near the end of the summer term to prepare for parents' evenings and transfer to the next class.

The problems

Because the need to plan for assessment had not been universally recognised, these records, although conscientiously constructed, were often completed without the child present. The judgements made by adults were, therefore, based on what they could remember of a child. This sometimes led to errors and a bit of guesswork!

There was no acknowledgement that assessment through observation takes time and planning, and must be done during sessions when the child is present. There was also little acceptance that these records should be used to affect planning. As there was no National Curriculum to shape judgements, the schedules matched the curriculum taught in the individual setting or school, and the records were difficult to transfer to another school or nursery.

What this method looks like now

Now we have a National Curriculum in each of the countries of the UK, we have national expectations for children at different stages of development, and a common framework for assessment. There is no longer a need for settings and schools to 'knit their own' assessment schedules, although of course the format for recording *is* still a decision for the individual setting.

The 'Let's screen everyone' model

This sort of assessment was often inspired by a manager or enthusiastic practitioner, or even a whole local authority, where there was a particular interest in finding out about reading, language development, spelling, or in compiling statistical evidence about groups or cohorts of children. There was a surge in the production of screening tests that could be used for whole groups or across a city or county, and these could be used, marked and analysed by schools and settings or the local authority (LA) themselves, rather than referring individual children to specialists. The statistics were often used to support applications for additional funding and to identify areas of deprivation or particular need.

The problems

These screenings were often used inappropriately across whole groups of children, where many didn't really need to be screened. There was pressure from national and local government departments to collect statistical data, and this tended to be their main use. There was sometimes a problem getting educational psychologists and other agencies to accept the results of these screenings as valid measures for individual children.

What this method looks like now

There have been two major influences on screening – one is that in the UK we now have national assessment procedures for the early years; the other has been the huge leap forward in identifying and responding to individual needs. The special needs Code of Practice and all the recent work on inclusion have raised practitioners' awareness of the individual child and the ways in which their needs can be met. Every child is now assessed in the early years using the framework of the curriculum, and the outcomes of this universal screening can now be used to assist learning for every child, and to support referrals for those whose development does not fall within the expected range. The check at two years, recently implemented in England, will add to the information available to settings and schools.

Coming to a common agreement

Fortunately, as national curriculum frameworks for teaching and learning have become more widespread, so have assessment methods. Each of these frameworks had their own assessment guidance and banks of statements for assessment guidance. The EYFS has formative assessment criteria in the Development Matters statements and summative assessment in the EYFS Profile. The other countries within the UK have also recognised the importance of coherent guidance across the whole range of early years experience. Although each variation may cover different parts of provision and periods of development, they all recognise the importance of assessment through observation, using clear criteria, and resulting in a holistic, child-focused process.

The future

Assessment will be with us for as long as early years professionals are interested in children as individuals, in watching them and 'catching them in the learning process'. It will remain while there are practitioners who are genuinely interested in what young children know and can do now, what they are interested in knowing and doing next, and how they, as adults, might help the child to do this.

> 'This does not mean pushing children too far or too fast, but instead meeting children where they are, showing them the next open door, and helping them to walk through it. It means being a partner with children, enjoying with them the power of their curiosity and the thrill of finding out what they can do.'
> *Learning, Playing and Interacting: Good practice in the Early Years Foundation Stage* (Department for Children, Schools and Families [DCSF], 2009)

Assessment is a fascinating, time-consuming activity, one that is a central responsibility of all practitioners. I hope the following chapters may also help you to make assessment an enjoyable, manageable and useful part of every day.

Introduction

Where did all this focus on assessment come from?

At the heart of any curriculum is the learning process. When children learn, they are constantly restructuring the connections between brain cells, making new links, reinforcing old ones, and pruning those that have ceased to be relevant. This process is both fascinating to watch (even from the outside) and extremely difficult to capture, particularly in the early years when brain-building is at its most complex and rapid. This is the reason why observation is the most important way to collect information, and that observations should be a daily component of planning and review of our work.

Professional assessment measures

Assessment is the attempt to capture and quantify a process, and is an activity undertaken by all conscientious professionals. Doctors assess what is wrong with their patients through diagnosis; advertisers assess how well their work promotes the products and services of those who employ them; builders assess the quality of their building methods and materials. A growing number of organisations and government led bodies use professional assessment measures to evaluate effectiveness in all areas of government spending.

Of course, many of these measures of success used in reports and the media are of 'outcomes', sometimes measured against externally set targets: how many people recover fully from operations? How many prisoners re-offend? How many children achieve the expected levels for their ages? How many bottles of shampoo have been sold? How much household waste has been recycled? These simple outcome measures are used to evaluate and sometimes undermine projects, businesses, manufacturers and individual performance all over the world. They are widely reported in the media and in research, particularly when making comparisons or reporting problems.

Early years programmes

Early years provision across the world has been under scrutiny and constant development over the past 50 years. Governments have been exploring and investing in the links between the quality of early years provision, future achievement in education, a successful economy, and social indicators such as crime and unemployment. Intervention programmes, funded by governments have sprung up across the world. These have a universal intention of enhancing the years before statutory schooling, supporting parents, and providing out-of-home pre-school care of high quality and maximum educational and social impact. Exploring the purposes and progress of some of these programmes makes interesting reading:

Head Start was initiated in the USA in 1965, with the intent to '*promote school readiness by enhancing the social and cognitive development of children through the provision of educational, health, nutritional, social and other services*'. The programme has now been in place for more than 40 years, and has attracted world-wide interest.

A whole range of schemes based on the Head Start model are now supported in countries across the world, and these included **Sure Start Children's Centres** in the UK, with an aim of '*giving children the best possible start in life*'. At the other end of the world, the **Te Whariki** ('a mat for all to stand on') early years curriculum, is a government initiative in New Zealand introduced in 1996 with the aim for children '*To grow up as competent and confident learners and communicators, healthy in mind, body, and spirit, secure in their sense of belonging and in the knowledge that they make a valued contribution to society*'. Even though it is such a recent innovation, Te Whariki is recognised world wide as a successful and well-documented approach where 'Learning Journeys' are the central feature of assessment.

Other education programmes based on individual philosophies, such as those of Rudolph Steiner or Maria Montessori; or in research into the way young children learn, such as High/Scope in the USA and the Reggio Emilia schools of Italy have their own unique assessment processes, as these originally functioned independently of government funding. Some remain entirely in the private sector, but others now receive some funding from governments, and are as accountable for standards as those in the state sector.

In England, any early years school or setting (including those in the private sector) can now apply for funding under the Nursery Education Grant provision for children under five, as long as they follow the curriculum for the early years (the EYFS) and assess children's progress towards the Early Learning Goals (ELG) and the EYFS Profile (EYFSP).

In each of the countries in the UK, as in many other countries, early years provision has become both a way of raising educational standards, and a way to engineer social change by improving both the education of children and the parenting skills of their families.

Programme success

The long-term success of Head Start programmes is still becoming evident 40 years after the original programme was devised. The change in children's futures has influenced politicians throughout the world who also wish to raise standards and to reduce the effects of social pressures on the poorest children. Impressive outcomes, collated in 1990, indicate that children who attended Head Start programmes, relative to their siblings who did not, are significantly more likely to complete high school, attend college, and possibly have higher earnings in their early twenties. They are less likely to have been booked or charged with a crime, and are more likely to have successful personal relationships. The educational outcomes of the programme are less well agreed, as there is some evidence that although there are significant benefits early on, the initial advantage of the programme is not sustained, and siblings who did not attend the Head Start programme soon catch up once they start school.

Of course, government funded early years programmes cost a great deal of taxpayers' money. They aim to provide high quality support and education, and with such expenditure inevitably there is accountability – usually in measures of improved outcomes matched to expenditure, or 'value for money'. These rely almost entirely on the collection of evidence through assessment by teachers and practitioners who know the children well.

The process of assessment

In 2002, when Tony Bertram and Chris Pascal undertook a review of early years provision in 20 countries across the world, they came to the following conclusions about the process of assessment in the early years:

> 'In most cases the assessment was achieved through the use of systematic teacher observation and scrutiny of the child's portfolio of activity.
> However, the use of ongoing assessment of children by class teachers and carers throughout the early years as a formative strategy for curriculum planning was almost universal. In most cases this was

actively encouraged at national level as a signal of good practice. This continuous, formative assessment was generally achieved through the use of a range of informal strategies, including observation, developmental checklists, videotapes, portfolios of children's activity, discussion with parents and the children themselves. Mostly, they were implemented and used at setting level, and formed the basis for curriculum planning and feedback reporting to parents.'

Early Years Education: An International Perspective, Tony Bertram and Chris Pascal (Centre for Research in Early Childhood, Birmingham UK, 2002)

This combination of assessment tools (systematic observation, coupled with scrutiny of portfolios of children's activities in photos and other recorded evidence) was and still is the most appropriate and the most effective way of finding out what children know and are able to do. That is why the notion of 'catching them at it' became the focus and the title for this book.

Every government-funded initiative is supported by written guidance on philosophy and practice, programmes of learning, and assessment frameworks and procedures. In the UK, government-driven systems have resulted in the Early Years Foundation Stage in England, The Foundation Phase in Wales, The Foundation Stage of Curriculum for Excellence in Scotland, and the Foundation Stage in Northern Ireland. They all have clear guidance on the value and process of assessment in the early years.

Defining observation and assessment

In England, the guidance contains helpful definitions of observation and assessment, and makes explicit the link between these and planning for learning.

'Ongoing assessment (also known as formative assessment) is an integral part of the learning and development process. It involves practitioners observing children to understand their level of achievement, interests and learning styles, and to then shape learning experiences for each child reflecting those observations.'
Statutory Framework for the Early Years foundation Stage (DFE, 2012)

It is gratifying to professionals that most governments, when evaluating the success of early years programmes, are now promoting assessment for learning, even though some are still tempted to take too much notice of simplistic data resulting from 'end of early years' summative assessment. We must thank the persistence and idealism of those education advisers close to governments for using their influence to secure the place of formative assessment through observation at the heart of their guidance to practitioners, and it is formative assessment, currently referred to as 'assessment for learning' (AfL) that will occupy the following chapters of this book.

Assessment for learning

In the rest of this book, I will be attempting to unscramble assessment for learning in the early years. This is the most complex sort of assessment – the assessment of *process*, where adults who work with young children look at learning in action, and then use the information to recognise successes and plan for the next steps. The Characteristics of Effective Learning, newly included in the EYFS, have helped practitioners to focus on this process, and guidance across the UK now includes detailed information to support assessment for learning.

This sort of assessment gives us the most useful and valuable information, but of course, like all good things, it is also the most time-consuming to collect and interpret. Young children are constantly on the move, both mentally and physically, and they are engaged in active learning which is notoriously difficult to pin down. Children know and can do things one day, then seem to have forgotten the next. They can demonstrate skills with one adult, but not with another. They use language at home that they seem unwilling to use in our settings and they behave in totally different ways with different children, in different places and even in different weather!

Keys to the assessment process

Practitioners and those who advise them know that there is a way of finding out what children really know and can do, and some of the keys to this process are:

- **Observing children systematically** in a range of places and situations, and particularly in child-initiated play where children really show what they can do.

'Assessments will be based primarily on observation of daily activities and events. Practitioners should note in particular the learning which a child demonstrates spontaneously, independently and consistently in a range of contexts.'
Early Years Foundation Stage Profile Handbook 2013 (DfE, 2012)

- **Providing an environment where children can follow their own interests** and practise the skills and activities that are important to them, not just to us; and being open to surprises and new learning, not just the objectives we have identified as adults.

'Children will become more deeply involved when you provide something that is new and unusual for them to explore, especially when it is linked to their interests.'
Development Matters in the EYFS (Early Education, 2012)

- **Talking with children** about their play and learning, asking questions, helping them to understand what they have learned, and what the next steps are for them; involving them as genuine partners in their learning.

'Give feedback and help children to review their own progress and learning. Talk with children about what they are doing, how they plan to do it, what worked well and what they would change next time.'
Development Matters in the EYFS (Early Education, 2012)

- **Involving all the adults in the setting**, as well as parents, carers and others who know the child.

'Parents and/or carers should be kept up-to-date with their child's progress and development. Practitioners should address any learning and development needs in partnership with parents and/or carers, and any relevant professionals.'
Statutory Framework for the Early Years Foundation Stage (DfE, 2012)

- **Collecting examples of learning in action**, using a range of techniques, including observation, portfolios and learning journeys, photos, examples of talk and discussion.

'Practitioners and EYFS Profile moderators should be aware that the definition of evidence is any material, knowledge of the child, anecdotal incident or result of observation or information from additional sources that supports the overall picture of a child's development. There is no requirement that it should be formally recorded or documented; the extent to which the practitioner chooses to record information will depend on individual preference. Paperwork should be kept to the

minimum that practitioners require to illustrate, support and recall their knowledge of the child's attainment.'
Early Years Foundation Stage Profile Handbook 2013 (DfE, 2012)

- **Using this information to identify what should happen next**, what should be planned, supported, offered or encouraged:

  'In planning activities, ask yourself: Is this an opportunity for children to find their own ways to represent and develop their own ideas?'
  Development Matters in the EYFS (Early Education, 2012)

Meeting children at the 'door to the next stage of learning', and genuinely helping them through it without pushing them too far or too fast, is the job of the skilled practitioners, as well as the central focus of this book.

The principles, purposes and audiences for assessment

1

If learning is so difficult to track, and assessment can give us such unreliable information, why do we do it? This book explores what we *must* do, what we *could* do, and what is manageable for us in our work.

In this chapter I will begin to explore the nature and principles of assessment:

- **What** is assessment? The clear definitions.
- **Why** should we do it? The principles we should stick to.
- **Who** is it for? The central audiences for our assessment work.

What is assessment?

When we talk generally about assessment, we usually encompass three processes – *assessment,* which is collecting information about learning; *recording* our assessment findings so we can make judgements about what has been learned and what needs to happen next; and *reporting* judgements to others. If we get the first two parts of the process right, the third will be both easy and useful.

Most assessment systems emphasise the key role played by observation in making the process reliable and useful, and this one is from the Revised Framework for the EYFS in England:

> 'Assessment plays an important part in helping parents, carers and practitioners to recognise children's progress, understand their needs, and to plan activities and support. Ongoing assessment (also known as formative assessment) is an integral part of the learning and development process. It involves practitioners observing children to understand their level of achievement, interests and learning styles, and to then shape learning experiences for each child reflecting those observations. In their interactions with children, practitioners should respond to their own day-to-day observations about children's progress, and observations that parents and carers share. Assessment should not entail

prolonged breaks from interaction with children, nor require excessive paperwork. Paperwork should be limited to that which is absolutely necessary to promote children's successful learning and development. Parents and/or carers should be kept up-to-date with their child's progress and development. Practitioners should address any learning and development needs in partnership with parents and/or carers, and any relevant professionals.'

Statutory Framework for the EYFS (DfE; 2012)

Of course, as practitioners observe, they contribute to this cycle – observe, assess, plan, exemplified in the diagram from Development Matters (Early Education):

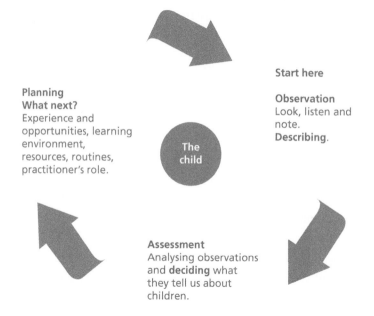

Start here

Observation
Look, listen and note.
Describing.

Planning
What next?
Experience and
opportunities, learning
environment,
resources, routines,
practitioner's role.

The
child

Assessment
Analysing observations
and **deciding** what
they tell us about
children.

So what is the connection between observation and assessment, record keeping and reporting?

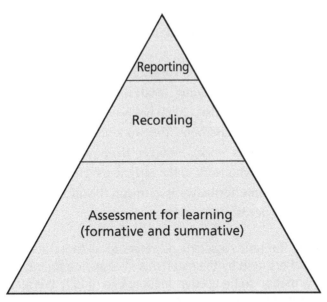

This diagram helps to clarify the three elements of assessment, recording and reporting, and is purposely divided into three unequal sections. Reading from the bottom of the triangle:

Assessment for Learning

The largest amount of space, time and attention should be given to the collection of evidence (*formative assessment or AfL*) almost entirely through observation, some of which may be written down. Recording, and then reporting condense the information into easily understood documentation, usually for a wider audience.

Recording

Drawing together these observations and other information and noting what this is telling us (*recording* in individual records or trackers) is a periodic activity, done perhaps every month or half term.

Reporting

Reporting is the final activity, undertaken every year (or sometimes more frequently, on change of school, for identifying progress against targets, or for seeking additional support for individual needs). This activity is selective. It dips into the rest of the process and selects key information to present for a particular purpose or audience. This smallest, most selective part of the process cannot give the depth or detail of the information on which it is based, and this is sometimes frustrating when misinterpreted.

Paul Black and Dylan William have worked in the field of assessment for learning for many years and their work, including 'Inside the Black Box' (2001) and 'Formative Assessment: Promises or problems?' (2007) has been very influential in defining and improving assessment in the classroom. This work has focused on schools (they use 'teacher' and 'student' in this work), however, their principles and definitions are also helpful to those of us who work in the early years. Here they define assessment, and how, in order to become 'formative assessment', the information must be used to adapt teaching to meet needs:

> 'In this paper, the term 'assessment' refers to all those activities under-taken by teachers, and by their students in assessing themselves, which provide information to be used as feedback to modify the teaching and learning activities in which they are engaged. Such assessment becomes 'formative assessment' when the evidence is actually used to adapt the teaching work to meet the needs.'
>
> *Inside the Black Box: Raising standards through classroom assessment*, Paul Black and Dylan William, King's College London School of Education (2001)

Black and William have also clarified the difference between assessment for learning, with its focus on promoting children's learning, and assessment primarily used for 'accountability, ranking or certifying competence':

> 'Assessment for learning is any assessment for which the first priority in its design and practice is to serve the purpose of promoting pupils' learning. It thus differs from assessment designed primarily to serve the purposes of accountability, or of ranking, or of certifying competence.
> An assessment activity can help learning if it provides information to be used as feedback, by teachers, and by their pupils in assessing themselves and each other, to modify the teaching and learning activities in which they are engaged. Such assessment becomes 'formative assessment' when the evidence is actually used to adapt the teaching work to meet learning needs.'
>
> *'The Nature and Value of Formative Assessment for Learning'*, Paul Black, King's College London School of Education (2004)

Children in the early years are active and inquisitive. They don't always learn things in a predictable order, and they show their learning through their faces, bodies and voices, not by answering written questions or by doing homework that can be marked. They also change during the day and the week, learning, forgetting, misunderstanding, connecting, practising and revisiting the things they are learning, piecing together the experiences they have each day, and sometimes making their own sense of what they have learned. Young children can also appear to understand, appear to be able to do something, appear to know stuff which we subsequently realise they have only partly grasped.

One thing practitioners learn very early in their work is that what may be described in books as an organised 'learning spiral' or web is in fact a much more complex process, more like the saying 'two steps forward, one step back, or even one step sideways' as the child revisits and reorganises pathways in their brain.

> 'No matter how meticulously we plan or what marvellous strategies we use during teaching, we can't reach inside learners' heads and put the learning there. There is a gap between learning and teaching that learners have to negotiate in order to construct new knowledge, skills and attitudes – albeit with our skilled input and help. We can't put learning in their heads!'
>
> *Assessment for learning: A Practical Guide* (Northern Ireland Curriculum); (The Council for the Curriculum, Qualifications and Assessment [CCEA], 2009)

Assessment in the UK

So, with the implementation of national frameworks for the early years in all four constituent countries of the UK, how is assessment described in early years guidance in these countries and how do these compare with countries across the world?

The Statutory Framework for the EYFS in England defines assessment as:

> 'Assessment plays an important part in helping parents, carers and practitioners to recognise children's progress, understand their needs, and to plan activities and support. Ongoing assessment (also known as formative assessment) is an integral part of the learning and development process. It involves practitioners observing children to understand their level of achievement, interests and learning styles, and to then shape learning experiences for each child reflecting those observations. In their interactions with children, practitioners should

respond to their own day-to-day observations about children's progress, and observations that parents and carers share.

Assessment should not entail prolonged breaks from interaction with children, nor require excessive paperwork. Paperwork should be limited to that which is absolutely necessary to promote children's successful learning and development. Parents and/or carers should be kept up-to-date with their child's progress and development. Practitioners should address any learning and development needs in partnership with parents and/or carers, and any relevant professionals.'

Statutory Framework for the EYFS (DfE; 2012)

The guidance on assessment in the Foundation Phase (three to seven) in Wales says:

'It is essential that practitioners working with children have an understanding of child development and the needs of children. By observing children carefully to note their progress, involvement and enjoyment, as well as focusing on the attainment of predetermined outcomes, practitioners should be able to plan a more appropriate curriculum that supports children's development according to individual needs.'

Observing Children (DCELLS, 2008)

In Northern Ireland, the guidance for pre-schools is:

'During the course of a busy day, it would be impossible to try to observe all that is going on. While adults will make observations as they arise naturally, it is important to draw a distinction between adults "being observant" and "planned observation", which has a clear focus. Planned observation should be included as part of the short-term planning and should identify specific opportunities where adults can talk with individual children, make observations during particular activities and ask questions.

Writing down notes from observations takes time, so only record useful information. Record significant observations as soon as they are made, as, in a busy day, it is all too easy to forget or overlook this information. Staff need to develop a method for ensuring that the information is recorded in a concise, systematic and manageable form. They may, for example, make and date observations in a notebook/diary or on sticky notes.'

Curricular Guidance for Pre-school Education (CCEA, 2008)

And for the Foundation Stage in Northern Ireland:

> 'It is important to view learning, teaching and assessment as a continuous cycle, where assessment is not the end point but should feed back into the process to help to improve learning. Since the purpose of teaching and the main purpose of assessment are to help children to learn, teaching and assessment need to be planned together as complementary aspects of the one activity. In turn, the information obtained from assessments should be used to inform the planning process.'
> *Understanding the Foundation Stage* (Northern Ireland) (CCEA, 2006)

In Scotland, the guidance is also clear and helpful. Key messages for assessment in the Early Years are:

- Assessment is an integral part of learning and teaching, and planning high quality learning activities for all children.
- Assessment provides an emerging picture of the child and their achievements, and can be a motivation for the child to do better and progress further in their learning.
- Assessment relates to the engagement of staff, children and parents, carers and the wider community in sharing and using a range of information to improve learning and development.

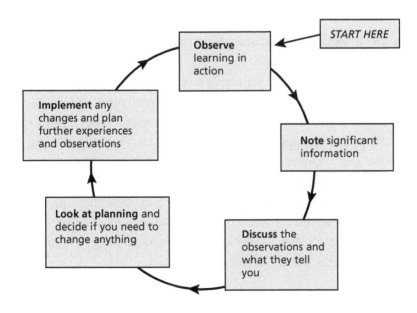

And in Curriculum for Excellence (Scotland):

> 'Assessment involves gathering, reflecting on and evaluating evidence of learning to enable staff to check on learners' progress.'
> *Curriculum for Excellence, Building the Curriculum 5: A Framework for Assessment* (The Scottish Government, 2010)

These examples all have observation at the heart of, and the start of the assessment process, and has a key influence on planning. The repeating daily, weekly and annual cycle of assessment and planning is at the centre of both learning and teaching in the early years, as this diagram explains:

The central guiding principle of assessment is that all assessments must be both *useful* and *used*. If we put this principle into action, our daily observations inform the next day's planning and provision; our weekly and monthly collections of evidence inform our medium-term planning, and of course our long-term consideration of children's learning, through annual reviews, reports and children's portfolios will influence our planning, organisation and provision for the following year.

The guidance for the Scottish Curriculum encapsulates this process in the following aide-memoir:

> 'Assessment needs to be planned as part of learning and teaching activities. In planning activities and experiences with young people, staff need to:
>
> - consider and share the outcomes towards which children and young people are working
> - use examples that illustrate standards and expectations
> - agree success criteria through discussion with each other and with learners
> - design learning experiences and activities that are likely to challenge and motivate and give opportunities to children and young people to provide evidence that demonstrates their knowledge and understanding, skills, attributes and capabilities
> - plan so that children and young people can show their thinking and provide evidence of what they have learned in response to planned experiences.'
> *Curriculum for Excellence, Building the Curriculum 5: A Framework for Assessment* (The Scottish Government, 2010).

Assessment across the world

Across the world, assessment systems for the early years have common messages. Here are some examples:

High/Scope settings use assessments developed for their own curriculum, and described in this way:

> 'With these tools, teachers, administrators and caregivers can monitor each child's developmental progress, plan appropriate daily activities based on observations recorded in anecdotal notes, and communicate effectively with parents and other important decision-makers about children's achievements.'
>
> *www.highscope.org*

In Reggio Emilia schools in Italy:

> 'Much attention is given to detailed observation and documentation of learning and the learning process takes priority over the final product. It is a model that demonstrates a strong relationship between educational establishment and community and provides a remarkable programme for professional development.'
>
> *(Quote from Learning and Teaching Scotland)*

In Te Whariki, the early years curriculum for New Zealand:

> Effective assessment is an everyday practice that involves noticing, recognising and responding to children's learning. It is formative in that it effects learning and teaching. It requires knowledgeable practitioners that understand children's learning. It includes and actively involves children and their families/whānau.'
>
> *www.educate.ece.govt.nz*

These definitions of assessment in the early years should lead us to thinking about the principles on which we base our practice in observing and assessing children's learning and asking why we should we do it.

The principles we should stick to

Principles are often the bit we skip over when reading or writing guidance for learning and teaching, but they are essential tools for checking why we are working in the way we do, and how well we are doing it. Assessment principles need to be agreed within each school or setting. Even if we discuss and then decide to adopt an existing set of principles such as those contained in local or national guidance for the early years, discussion within the team confirms a shared commitment and helps to establish a coherent approach to the process.

Sometimes the principles for assessment are stated within an overall statement of curriculum principles, such as these from High/Scope:

> 'The five basic principles – active learning, positive adult-child interactions; a child-friendly learning environment; a consistent daily routine; and team-based daily child assessment – form the framework of the High/Scope approach.'
> *Educating Young Children: Active Learning Processes for Preschool and Childcare Programs*; Mary Hohmann and David P. Weikart (High/Scope Publications, 2002)

These overarching but simple principles guide all the work in High/Scope settings and schools, giving everyone a framework for their practice.

As in High/Scope, national guidance for the early years curriculum in countries throughout the world always makes mention of assessment, often amplified in specific principles for assessment in separate documentation on assessment. For instance, the government in England has previously issued several volumes of guidance on assessment, rooted in the following eight assessment principles.

I have followed each of the principles with some questions to lead your thinking and your team's discussion of practice in your setting:

1 **Assessment must have a *purpose*.**
   Points to think about: Are our assessments purposeful? Do we know why we are doing them? Who and what are they for?

2 ***Observation* of children participating *in everyday activities* is the most reliable way to build up an accurate picture of what children know, understand, feel, are interested in and can do.**
   Points to think about: Do we make most of our assessments through observation? Do we have a clear system to make sure we observe every child regularly? Do we observe activities that the children have really chosen for themselves?

3 **All practitioners should** *be ready to capture spontaneous but important moments in the day, but some* **observations should be** *planned.*
Points to think about: How well do we plan for assessment, so we are not feeling under pressure? How much time do we allocate to watching children? How systematic is our observation process? What is the balance between planned observations and capturing spontaneous moments? How do we use the observations to help with planning?

4 **Judgement of children's development and learning should be** *based on skills, knowledge, understanding and behaviour that they demonstrate consistently* **and** *independently.*
Points to think about: Do we do observations of child-initiated activities often enough? Can we be sure that our assessment of each child recognises evidence from different activities, in different places and with different companions?

5 **An effective assessment will take into account** *all aspects of a child's development and learning.*
Points to think about: Does our assessment programme recognise all aspects of the child and the curriculum? Do we recognise and include particular strengths and interests of individuals? Do we collect enough information out of doors? Are we truly focusing on the 'whole child'?

6 **Accurate assessment will also take into account** *contributions from a range of perspectives.*
Points to think about: Do we include contributions from all colleagues – teaching assistants, nursery nurses and officers, representatives from outside agencies such as speech therapy and so on?

7 *Parents and other primary carers should be actively engaged* **in the assessment.**
Points to think about: Do we include and value contributions from parents and carers? How easy is it for them to tell us what they know?

8 *Children should be fully involved* **in their own assessment.**
Points to think about: Do we include and value contributions from children themselves? Are these valued as much as contributions from adults?

Take a moment to think about some of the assessments you make in your work, and look at them with these principles in mind. How well are you doing in your setting?

Clear principles help practitioners to make the assessment process both manageable and meaningful for adults and children, providing useful information, which is well used to shape future experiences – an essential key to successful practice. Any assessment you make should give you useful information which contributes to the picture of the whole child that you are building up. However, if you don't use the information you have collected, you are wasting time collecting it! Every time you plan an assessment activity, ask yourself these two key questions: Does this assessment give me useful information? *And* do I use this information to improve the provision for the child?

Here are some examples of how the balance can vary between 'useful assessment' and 'assessment properly used'. How would you respond to each of these examples?

> *Example 1: A practitioner collects pages of information from parents at pre-admission home visits. She carefully copies her notes onto a form and files them in a beautiful ring binder in her cupboard and never refers to it again.* This potentially useful information is NEVER used!

> *Example 2: Another practitioner is asked by her manager to use the EYFS Profile statements to assess the three year olds in her group. These assessments are scrutinised by the manager who creates complex charts of 'progress made' and 'attainment' for each child.* Using an assessment schedule intended for five year olds to assess the learning of three year olds does NOT provide useful information, but it is used as if it did!

> *Example 3: A group of practitioners in a pre-school frequently make mental notes and jottings as they work and play alongside the children. At the end of every day they meet and discuss the significant things they have seen, and what they might do on the following day to improve their provision.* These are USEFUL assessments, professionally USED.

Who is assessment for?

As mentioned earlier in this chapter, assessment needs clarity in both the *purpose* (in the principles and processes) and *audience* (in the feedback process to children and adults). We have to know why are we assessing and who it is for.

As you will see from the principles for assessment, there has been an increasing emphasis on involving colleagues, parents and carers, and children themselves in assessment activities.

> 'Accurate assessments take account of contributions from a range of perspectives including the child, their parents and other relevant adults.'
> *Early Years Foundation Stage Profile Handbook*
> (Standards and Testing Agency, 2012)

Of course, children and their parents are the key audiences in our day-to-day assessment processes, but, when we consider all the information, we discover a whole range of groups needing to be both involved and informed about assessment. Here are some:

- children
- parents, carers and families
- practitioners in the setting or school
- managers and heads of settings and schools
- governors of schools
- outside agencies such as therapists and special needs services
- local authority personnel
- inspectors
- local and national government.

It is possible, but not always easy, to give all these groups a sense of involvement in the *process* by listening carefully and involving them in the setting.

It is quite another thing when you consider the *outcomes* of assessment. Each of the groups needs different sorts of information, presented to them in ways they can understand. Parents need and want information about their own child, in language they can understand, and years of research has shown that they are centrally interested in two things – 'Is my child happy?' and 'Are they getting on as well as they could?' Local and national governments are particularly interested in simple statistics that describe cohort (year group) or school/setting averages and general standards. Inspectors are interested in both the process and the outcomes of assessment, and as their visits are now so brief, they need this in easily digested form.

Of course it is easy to forget that children need feedback too, and a sense of involvement in how they are doing, and this principle is at the heart of assessment for learning. Children need support and praise for success, but they also need opportunities to stop and think about what they are learning, and helpful feedback on where they are and what they need to do to improve. As one teacher has put it:

> 'The children's minds are focused on what they are learning, especially during play-based learning, so we try to pause between activities and ask "Can anyone tell me something new they've learned?"'

And of course practitioners need the whole picture, not just assessing because they have been told to, but using the information from every observation and every assessment to improve provision, and involving everyone in the process, not just the outcomes. Nobody has ever pretended that the job is easy, and the more you try, the more difficult it seems to be to get the whole process right for everyone.

Here are some examples of the work of practitioners, some is principled assessment, some is less so. As you read the examples, ask yourself 'Who are these assessment processes for?'

Are they for the children, the adults, for both or no-one?

- Rory (age four) is involved in taking regular photos of his work and the activities he likes. Once he has taken the photos they are printed by his key person, Rosie, who sticks them in his record book, but never discusses them with him. Rory is never involved in talking about why he took the photos, what they tell him or other people about his choices, or what he might do next with these favourite resources.
- Keran (age four) also takes photos regularly. He downloads them onto the computer, prints them himself, shows them at group sessions and tells the other children why he took them. He puts some of them in his virtual portfolio (a computer based collection of photos for each child, sometimes annotated with his own words, typed in by a practitioner) and takes printed versions home, where he tells his parents all about them.
- Kelly plans an activity for her key children for group time every day, matching the activities carefully to children's interests and abilities. When the activity is complete, Kelly sends the children off to play and then writes brief notes about what has happened during the activity. She uses these to plan the next day's work.
- Meena plans activities for her key group. As she works with the children she gives them frequent feedback about what they are doing, asking open questions, giving clear praise for success and making notes on her

notepad as she works. At the end of the session she makes time to talk to the children about what she has written, talking with them about what went well and how the children could develop or improve their skills. She involves the children in deciding what they need to do next, and plans this for the next day.

Are they for the practitioners, the parents or the children?

- In Matthew's setting, practitioners use sticky notes for jottings of things they notice during the day. They put these in individual children's files at the end of the session, and visit each child's page after the children have left, as they check that what they have planned for the next day is still meeting the needs of the children. The discussion includes informal observations, which have not always been written down. These indicate children's current interests, schema play and changing friendships. The next morning, the files are available for parents to read if they wish, and many do. A pack of sticky notes is placed near the files, so parents can comment too.
- In Sarah's setting the sticky notes are carefully linked to the six areas of the curriculum. These are also put in individual children's files, but informal observations are not discussed and the files are not available for parents to look at. Parents' comments are not included in day-to-day assessment, although they are always asked to comment on their child's annual report.

Are they for the managers or the practitioners?

- At the beginning of the year, Cara is asked by her manager to produce targets for numeracy and literacy for each of the children in her Reception class, using the end of year statements in the curriculum (the EYFS Profile). The manager checks progress against these targets each half term, using samples of children's work and her own observations, and then produces a chart of progress against the targets, which is used as part of Sarah's Performance Review. Sarah does not refer to the targets between annual performance reviews.
- Marta assesses each child in her Reception class during the first two weeks of the autumn term. She uses these assessments to set simple targets in three areas of learning – 'talking and listening', 'getting on with others', and 'independent learning'. These targets are discussed with the children, and

each child has the targets in the front of their workbook, which they use for photos and recorded work. Marta sends copies of the targets to each child's parents, with an invitation to discuss these if they wish. She also gives a copy to her team leader, and keeps another in her planning folder to help with grouping, with her planning, and with differentiating activities. Marta also refers to the targets regularly as she observes the children and talks to them. When a target is met, there is celebration in the class and at home. Targets are reviewed formally every half term and renewed or adjusted according to each child's needs.

Take a bit of time to think about how each of these practitioners has responded to the need for everyone to know what is happening. Involving everyone is a time-consuming and sometimes frustrating job, but well managed it can be very rewarding and can result in better learning and better teaching.

Assessment in practice – the nuts and bolts

2

Once our principles are agreed, and we have identified our audiences we can begin to unpick the practicalities of assessment, and make daily and weekly decisions about space, time and energy for the process, and for following the leads presented by looking at learning.

Further chapters in this book will explore in more depth the 'how' of assessment, by identifying a range of ways of assessing learning, from informal observation which may not even be written down, to formal tests such as those used to identify children's additional learning needs. Here I will refer to the broad range of tasks around the timing, planning and methodology of the whole assessment process, including recording and reporting.

When is assessment done?

If we return to the diagram in the previous chapter, we can now begin to add some details to the process.

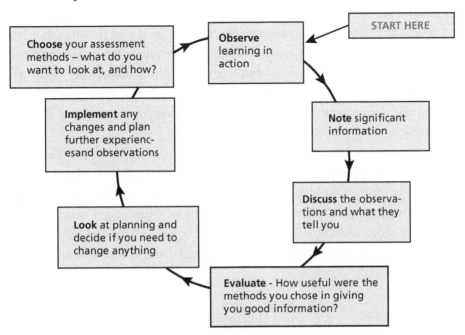

It is easy to overlook the 'how' and 'when' stages of this process, assuming that we can find out everything we need to know about learning by one method, or that everything is fine when we only look at a small proportion of what is going on. It is also very tempting to think we will find time to observe and assess children's learning without actually allocating any time for it in our day and week.

Consider these examples:

- **The baby room:** the practitioners in the baby room wanted to give the children more immediate individual choice of the toys and other resources in the room, instead of putting out the toys they thought the babies would like. They decided to monitor the gestures and 'eye pointing' of individual children, giving the babies any toy they indicated. This seemed to give the babies many more opportunities to choose the toy they wanted, and most of them seemed much happier and played for longer with their chosen toys.

    However two babies still seemed unhappy and restless until one practitioner said 'It's no good just letting them choose from the ones they can see, some of the toys are in the cupboard. I know Jamie really likes the musical toys and he can't see them!' This comment, based on informal knowledge of a child in her key group helped all the staff to understand that babies may need to be carried round the room, including looking in open and closed cupboards so they can have a genuine choice of all the toys on offer.

- **The book corner:** Julie and her Reception team wanted to know why the book corner was under-used during free choice time. They looked at all their observations and found that they had very little information about the use of this space. They decided to systematically observe the use of this area, but knew that if one of them went to sit there, children would automatically come too! They decided to use a more subtle method of observation. They drew up an observation schedule, and Julie looked up every five minutes from whatever she was doing to jot down who was in the book corner and what they were doing.

    After a few days, the team looked at the information and found that far from being under-used, the book corner was visited by the majority of children over these days, although they sometimes didn't stay very long. The practitioners decided to ask the children what would make the book corner more inviting and comfortable for a longer stay. The children really enjoyed being involved in the improvements, and the result was that they really did stay longer.

- **ICT experiences:** Laura has a key group of three and four year olds, and she wanted to check their experiences of ICT. She made a list of all the equipment, such as the photocopier, digital camera, light box, computer and so on. She added a picture of the equipment to each item on the list, then called the children to her one at a time, asking them if they knew what each one was and how to use it. Most of the children were able to name the equipment, and some could explain in words and gestures something about how to use it, but it didn't give Laura much evidence of the sorts of experiences they had had or the skills they had acquired.

  When she had talked to four of the children she decided that the information she was getting was of no real use to her, so she stopped using this method and planned to set up some specific activities with ICT equipment that she could observe and photograph in action. This gave her much more useful information, and she was able to discuss the activities with each child, getting even more information, including their use and understanding of technical language.

The practitioners' stories told above all describe professional attempts to 'capture' the effectiveness of their provision. Each one has given time and thought to what they are doing, and we would recognise their commitment to the process.

So how do we choose the methods and plan the time for that crucial observation of children, particularly when they are engrossed in activities they have chosen themselves?

Ten tips for assessment

Managing the process of assessment, day-to-day and week-by-week is central to its success. Here are *ten tips* for making the process manageable when you are planning for assessment, with some excerpts from guidance to expand each one:

Tip 1: Commit yourselves
Make a team commitment to observation, write a small statement of intent, such as:

We all know the importance of observing learning, and we commit ourselves to a balanced programme of informal assessments, written observations and other means such as discussion, taking photos, listening to children talking etc. This will ensure that every child's strengths and interests are recognised, and their achievements across the whole curriculum are acknowledged.

If you have made a commitment in writing, you are much more likely to keep to it.

Tip 2: Know your percentages

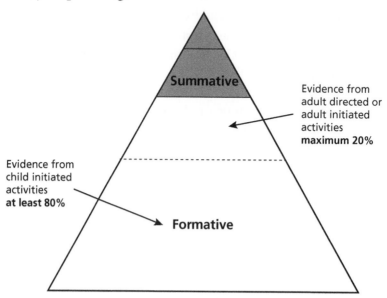

This version of our original assessment triangle clarifies the percentages generally agreed to be relevant when observing young children.

Practitioners are always anxious to know how, when and where they should be making ongoing assessments of individuals. The EYFS Profile Handbook (2013) gives much helpful advice, and this is explored in more detail in later sections of this book, but it is worth quoting briefly here:

> 'Assessments will be based primarily on observation of daily activities and events. Practitioners should note in particular the learning which a child demonstrates spontaneously, independently and consistently in a range of contexts. Accurate assessment will take account of a range of perspectives including those of the child, parents and carers and other adults who have significant interactions with the child.'
> Early years Foundation Stage Profile Handbook 2013 (Standards and Testing Agency; DFE; 2012)

And:

> 'The majority of evidence for EYFS Profile judgements will come from the practitioner's knowledge of the child gained from observation of the child's self-initiated activities. In addition, some adult-led activities will offer insight into children's attainment, where they have the opportunity to demonstrate what they know, understand and can do.
>
> Much evidence will be gleaned from day to day interactions with children as practitioners build up their knowledge of what children know and can do, for assessment purposes and to inform future practice and provision. This evidence, often not formally recorded, provides the basis on which judgements are made and the focus of a moderation dialogue.'
>
> Early years Foundation Stage Profile Handbook 2013 (Standards and Testing Agency; DFE; 2012)

This focus on independent activity, child-initiated learning and the inclusion of the new Characteristics of Effective Learning has ensured that practitioners take time to observe every child engaged in independent activities, to establish what the child can do unaided, and to find out about interests and abilities that are not always evident in adult-directed activities. Some practitioners had previously missed the opportunities offered by such observations. They had taken advantage of children's enthusiasm for their own interests and choices to concentrate instead on adult-led group work, to read with children or to work with those who have additional learning or language needs, largely missing the information offered by watching children as they follow their own interests.

Tip 3: Know your stuff and balance your methods

There are many ways of observing and recording learning, and of giving feedback to children on how they are doing. You will already know some of them, and in Chapter 00 there are descriptions of many more, and the advantages and disadvantages of each. As you consider and adopt new methods remember to always ask yourself 'Why am I doing this, and what do I want to find out?' –principled assessment. Some of the time (but not more than 20 per cent) may be used to collect evidence through adult-led tasks and activities, but many practitioners find that they can collect all the information they need through careful planning and organisation of the environment, reflecting on what they observe, and adjusting planning to meet the changing needs and interests of the children. This is now described as responsible pedagogy:

'Responsible pedagogy enables each child to demonstrate learning in the fullest sense. It depends on the use of assessment information to plan relevant and motivating learning experiences for each child. Effective assessment can only take place when children have the opportunity to demonstrate their understanding, learning and development in a range of contexts.

Children must have access to a rich learning environment which provides them with the opportunities and conditions in which to flourish in all aspects of their development. It should provide balance across the areas of learning. Integral to this is an ethos which respects each child as an individual and which values children's efforts, interests and purposes as instrumental to successful learning.'
Early years Foundation Stage Profile Handbook 2013 (Standards and Testing Agency; DFE; 2012)

Tip 4: Make time

It has been said that if you are not spending at least 20 per cent of *your* time observing the children as they work and play independently, then you are not doing enough assessment. This figure (the equivalent of one day a week) may seems horrific, but before you put this book down and go rushing around in a panic, remember that there are a huge number of activities that constitute assessment. You are 'doing assessment' when:

- you stop what you are doing and watch a group or a single child, storing away what you see in your mind, and adding it to the information already there
- you ask a child a question and listen carefully to the answer
- you check with a parent to confirm that a young child is consistently using her left hand at home as she is at nursery
- you make a note to check again the child who doesn't seem to be understanding the concept of 'more and less'
- you ask your colleague to work with a small group of children who appear to be having difficulty using scissors
- you share a book with a child, encouraging them to take turns with you in reading
- you join a group of children in the construction area, working alongside them, discussing what is happening and observing how they are working.

All these, and many more are assessment activities, and these take up time even when you do them on a professional 'autopilot' as many multi-tasking professionals do. Most practitioners are observing and assessing progress with part of their brain during the whole session, and many are almost unconsciously adjusting what they do in the light of what they see. Of course it would save a lot of time if we could do all our assessment work in the background as we do other things, but time spent in close observation, noting or just remembering what we see, and discussing this with others is one of the most important professional activities. When we give time to observations, we sometimes feel:

- guilty that we aren't 'teaching'
- harassed when we never have enough time to do everything anyway
- or as if we aren't doing our jobs properly when we are sitting with a clipboard, talking with children, or just looking at how things are going.

We *must* stop feeling guilty, and support each other in this vital part of our role. It is vital to set aside parts of the day when you will be consciously and systematically gathering evidence of children's learning. These will include being clear about what an observer is expected to do (a job description for observers!) and making sure you include these elements in your planning:

- watching children in self-initiated play
- planned observations of individual 'focus children'
- leaving time at the end of adult-led activity sessions to reflect on and sometimes jot down significant information
- arranging for your colleague to observe particular children as you lead plenary or group times
- producing and trying out simple schedules for tracking activities or individuals
- giving enough time for 'longer recorded observations' of activities, individuals or groups
- identifying objectives or intentions from your long or medium-term planning which you intend to observe
- observing and providing for children's emerging interests
- talking with individuals and groups
- talking with parents and colleagues about individual children, so you get a range of views.

Tip 5: Acknowledge when things aren't working

This might, for example, mean realising that your presence in an activity is altering the behaviour of the children; discussing whether doing all your observations on the same day of the week is giving you the right balance of information; or abandoning a simple schedule that is easy to fill in, but gives no useful data. A vital professional activity is looking at what you are doing, and making sure it is an effective use of your time.

Tip 6: Look for the learning, not just what you expect

If all your planned observations and assessments are carefully focused on individual objectives (or intentions), it is very tempting to ignore all the other information that the children are offering you. Be open to other information, note this as well as what you planned or expected, use the time to look broadly, while not forgetting your original focus.

> 'Some observations will be planned but some may be a spontaneous capture of an important moment. It is likely that observations of everyday activities will provide evidence of attainment in more than one area of learning.
>
> Observational assessment does not require prolonged breaks from interaction with children, nor excessive written recording. It is likely to be interwoven with high quality interactions or conversations in words or sign language with children about their activities and current interests.'
>
> *EYFS Profile Handbook 2013; DFE*

This takes practice – it is easy to be distracted!

Tip 7: Share the load

Observational assessment is very time consuming, so it is vital to use other people to help with this important job. Everyone in the setting can and should be involved. Practitioners (teachers, teaching assistants, nursery nurses and nursery officers) all have a real contribution to make, particularly because they can give a new perspective on the child or the activity. Students, volunteers, parents and other visitors often see your setting in a different light and can make useful comments on what they see. And of course, the children themselves can open our eyes to what is important to them.

Tip 8: Be out of doors as well as inside

Observations of children in the outside area, and on walks, trips and visits will give you a new view of what interests them, what they can do and who they like to play with. These observations will enable you to value the whole child; and for some children, the outdoors is the only place where they can really be themselves. Individual children have differing needs and interests, which practitioners must take into account, and among these is the need to be out of doors:

> '…there may be children who are at an earlier stage of development than others in the cohort; some may have summer birthdays. These children and others may be highly active and more likely to demonstrate what they know, understand and can do in situations which are sympathetic to this inclination, often outdoors.'
> EYFS Profile Handbook 2013; Standards and Testing Agency

Tip 9: Know and note what's significant

It is easy to spend a lot of time writing down everything you see, or what a child is doing for every minute. Looking carefully for what is important (significant) in what you see is an art, and takes time to learn. One practitioner described this as 'instant editing'. She follows the advice 'watch for five minutes, then write what is significant about what you have just seen'. This helps her to focus and distill what she is seeing.

Tip 10: Follow the children

When you are observing child-initiated learning, don't be tempted to say 'I'll go and watch Bonnie in the home corner'. Bonnie will almost certainly decide not to go to the home corner, or to leave it as soon as you arrive, so it's important to be flexible and follow them. Otherwise, how can you possibly know what you need to do next?

How is assessment used?

Once you have agreed your principles, it is vital to agree on how you will use the information you have collected.

At the beginning of this chapter I recommended that assessment should be both useful and used, and this statement might seem obvious, but asking yourself why you do observations, ask questions or set challenges for children is an important part of the job. Assessment is not only important in accountability to the government or your managers, it has a vital contribution to make to the job of an early years practitioner.

Assessment can also be used to:

- **Feed back to individuals**

  An example: *Martha told the children at group time that she had seen Garry and Shaun doing something very interesting, using chalk to make up a monster counting game on the stepping-stones in the garden. She invited the boys to tell the other children about their game and how to play it. Next day, several other children joined the boys in their game. Martha joined in too.*

  Assessment information is most useful when the key findings are fed back appropriately to the person who is being assessed. This does *not* mean you have to feed back every observation to every child, but you should be building in some reference to your observations when you discuss activities with individuals and groups.

- **Ensure that the curriculum is meeting the needs of the children**

  An example: *Paula was observing a small group of children in the garden, looking for evidence of effective learning, and particularly of children 'having their own ideas, finding ways to solve problems, and find new ways of doing things' from Creating and Thinking Critically. She could not find much evidence for this, and soon realised why. The adults put all the equipment out for the children, and controlled their use of it by strict rota systems. The children couldn't access the equipment independently, only when the adults told them it was their turn. She recommended to the other staff that they should find a way of letting the children have more freedom to select and use the resources independently.*

  Assessment should help you to see if the activities and resources you are offering to the children help them to learn the things you want them to know.

- **Ensure that you are meeting the needs of every child in your group, particularly those with additional needs and children who do not have English their first language**

  An example: *The manager of the nursery asked Clare to observe a new child who seemed to have very limited English, to check that he was getting access to a range of activities. Clare observed him over two days and found that despite his limited English, he was in fact getting involved in a whole range of activities, even though he could not always make himself understood.*

  Assessment should give you information about children with additional needs, and how you are meeting these needs.

- **Enhance opportunities for learning through continuous provision**
  An example: *Caran and her colleagues spent a day looking at whether the resources for play in their setting gave children opportunities to find out more about pirates (their current centre of interest) during child-initiated time. They watched role play, games outside, the book corner, the workshop and mark-making areas to check. They found that children were using the role-play resources and the pirate books to extend their ideas about pirates, but there was no use of the workshop and mark-making areas.*
  They decided to draw children's attention to the objects pirates use (telescopes, treasure chests, treasure maps etc) and to offer some suitable resources in the mark-making and workshop areas to stimulate their interest. They added cardboard tubes, pictures of treasure maps, boxes for treasure chests, gold foil and other resources to the existing range. Further observations showed that the new resources had inspired children to expand their play and use all the areas of the room.

  Observation helps you to find out whether children are using the resources you are offering to reinforce and extend knowledge and skills through their current interests.

- **Monitor teaching and learning**
  An example: *Paul was responsible for the fine motor skills development of the children in the nursery. He regularly checked their progress by planning and observing an adult-led activity, such as cutting along a line, threading beads, picking up small objects with tweezers, finger painting and so on. He logged children's progress on a simple tick sheet to indicate whether they could do the task easily/with some difficulty/with great difficulty/not at all. He used the observation evidence to plan further fine motor skills practice in self-initiated and adult-led sessions.*

  Assessment information is useful in deciding whether what you are planning and teaching is what children are learning!

- **Track children's activities and interests to find out who is doing what, and when**
  An example: *Four weeks after she moved into her group, Maddy's key person, Shelpa, was updating the children's records. She found that she had less information about Maddy than the other children in her group, and felt that she didn't know Maddy's interests and friends very well. So Shelpa*

spent a day quietly tracking her and logging where Maddy was and what she was doing every 15 minutes, but without Maddy knowing. When Shelpa looked at the tracking information, she found that Maddy spent most of her time alone or on the edge of groups, watching the other children. Shelpa decided to join Maddy sometimes, to help her to enter play situations and make friends.

Assessment information should give you information about how individuals use the resources and activities you offer.

- **Monitor the use, access and participation in activities, resources and spaces**
  An example: *The practitioners in a pre-school felt that the girls were not choosing to play in the blocks or in the construction area. They talked about whether this was important, and agreed that block and construction play could offer opportunities that other areas of the setting could not. Firstly they watched the children informally and found that their impression was right, girls rarely chose to play in these areas. They tried an experiment. They put a box of play people in the block area, and took turns to join construction play, modelling how a female could build and construct too. This worked very well – girls and boys joined them and used the new resources to play with greater complexity as they told stories about the characters.*

  Assessment can give you information about whether the activities you offer are being accessed by all the children. We sometimes assume that if we plan or offer something, all the children will experience it.

Of course, we could get so obsessed with assessment and spend so much time doing it that there is no time left to teach! Effective settings and effective professionals work hard to get the balance right between teaching and learning, and assessment, making sure that they plan enough time for assessment, but not too much. These effective practitioners are very clear about what they *must* do (because it is the law); what they *could* do to set the legal requirements in an assessment framework that is really useful to everyone; and what is useful to them, to the children, to their families and to other professionals.

An exploration of the legal requirements comes in the next chapter, and is followed by chapters on the EYFS Profile, assessment and recording methods.

What are my legal responsibilities?

3

What are the requirements?

The *requirements* are those things that practitioners in the early years in each country or each education system *must* do, they are enshrined in law, in employment contracts and in the conditions attached to local or national government funding. Relevant legislation for safeguarding children's welfare when they are out of their parents' care is set down in national documentation, along with the legal requirements for the curriculum and its assessment. In England, these are all collected and neatly presented together in the *Statutory Framework for the Early Years Foundation Stage* (DFE, 2012).

Any statement including the word 'must' is likely to be a legal requirement, and I have underlined this word when it is used. Those statements containing the words 'should' or 'might' (also underlined in the following text) are likely to indicate guidance on something practitioners and settings could do if they wish, if their setting decides to, or if they are advised to. Some of this guidance is generated in local government (local authorities in England) and is intended to help practitioners to interpret the legislation.

Increasingly, the guidance for the EYFS in England has been outsourced to early years *organisations, such as Early Education* (www.early-education.org.uk*), Foundation* Years (www.foundationyears.org.uk), or (foundations@4Children.org. uk) leaving the DFE website for the publication of documents describing legal requirements. Guidance documents are intended to be helpful, but it is important to understand the difference between statements containing the word 'must' and those indicating 'should/might' which can make the guidance seem more like requirements. It is important to be clear about what you *must* do and check it regularly!

In general **requirements** are things that a practitioner must do:

1 because there is **legislation that affects everyone in the country**, such as health and safety, equality of opportunity, anti-discrimination, or employment law;

2 because the **government** requires those who work with children to do them if they work in the state education system;

3 because **their employer** requires their employees to undertake them if they work in a private or independent nursery or school;

4 or because **their employer has accepted a state regulation** as a condition of receiving state funding or grant aid.

Because early years provision in the UK, and particularly in England, is so diverse in type, size and scope, understanding the requirements for assessment, recording and reporting in the country where you work becomes even more important. In this chapter, we concentrate on the requirements for practitioners working in state funded education provision England, in the private, voluntary and independent sectors, which are a condition of receiving government funding through the Nursery Education Grant. The requirements in England are described here in brief, with a further chapter on the details of the processes of the newly implemented Two Year Old Check and the EYFS Profile at the end of the Foundation Stage.

In a book like this, the descriptions can only give an overview of processes and of legislation. Practitioners should make sure they know what their responsibilities are, and update their own knowledge regularly (ideally at least once a year!). The details of assessment requirements for all schools in England, whatever their status, are contained in the Assessment and Reporting Requirements (ARA) published annually by the Standards and Testing Agency.

NB If you work in another country in the UK, or abroad, even in a British International School, or if you work in an Academy or Free School, you will need to be clear about your specific responsibilities, as there will be variations.

In England, information about the requirements for the curriculum and for assessment is set out in four areas:

- the curriculum entitlement for every child *and*

The requirements for:

- assessment
- recording
- reporting to parents and carers, including the information sent to the next school or setting.

For ease of reference, the assessment, recording and reporting requirements for England are presented here in sequenced sections:

1 The requirements for assessment during the EYFS – from birth to five years.
2 The overall requirements for assessment at the end of the EYFS (the end of Reception year, the year in which the child becomes five and transfers to Key Stage 1).
3 The requirements for record keeping during the EYFS.
4 The requirements for annual reports to parents during the EYFS.

1. The requirements for assessment during the EYFS

These requirements are taken from the *Statutory Framework for the Early Years Foundation Stage* (DFE; 2012). This is the latest version of the Statutory Framework for the EYFS, and it has some significantly different statutory requirements from previous versions.

The first is the implementation of the Progress Check at Age Two, which is described as follows:

> 'When a child is aged between two and three, practitioners *must* review their progress, and provide parents with a short summary of their child's development in Prime areas (Communication, Personal, Social and Emotional, and Physical development). This progress check *must* identify the child's strengths, and any areas where the child's progress is less than expected.
>
> Practitioners *must* discuss with parents and/or carers how the summary of development can be used to support learning at home.
>
> Practitioners *must* agree with parents and/or carers the most useful point to provide the summary (it is suggested, although not required, that the summary should inform the Healthy Child Programme health and development review carried out by health visitors).
>
> Providers *must* have the consent of parents and/or carers to share information directly with other relevant professionals.'
>
> *Statutory Framework for the EYFS: (DfE, 2012)*

The requirement is for a written check, but there is no statute about what the written check must contain, beyond that described above. Some guidance has been issued to help practitioners with this process, but this is not statutory, and settings are encouraged to develop their own models. During the period from birth to five, the Two Year Old check, and the Early Years Foundation Stage Profile are the only prescribed assessment requirements.

Before, beyond and around this, practitioners *must* observe the children and respond to what they see, so they can help children make progress. There is no requirement of how much time should be spent on observation; how much should be written down; how much the parents should be told and when, how or even whether the observation evidence should be kept. The requirement is that between birth and five, observations should be used to help children make progress towards the 17 revised Goals for early learning, and to inform parents of their progress and any difficulties.

Development Matters (Early Education; 2012) has also been updated in line with the revised Framework. This document has detailed guidance on the expectations at each stage of development, and in each of the seven areas of learning and development. This guidance also offers helpful advice on the observation and assessment of the Characteristics of Effective Learning. Practitioners are now expected to expand their assessments by including observations of the child's development in these characteristics, so that at the end of the reception year, practitioners can use this information to summarise development using the EYFS Profile:

The EYFS Profile summarises and describes children's attainment at the end of the EYFS. It is based on ongoing observation and assessment in the three prime and four specific areas of learning, and the three learning characteristics, set out below:

The prime areas of learning:

- communication and language
- physical development
- personal, social and emotional development

The specific areas of learning:

- literacy
- mathematics
- understanding the world
- expressive arts and design

The learning characteristics:

- playing and exploring
- active learning
- creating and thinking critically

A completed EYFS Profile consists of 20 items of information: the attainment of each child assessed in relation to the 17 ELG descriptors, together with a short narrative describing the child's three learning characteristics.

– here is no statutory requirement to record all your observations, but children's curricular records should provide information that helps parents and others to understand the pace and unique nature of each child's development. Such evidence will include photographs, short notes made by all the adults who have regular contact with the child, and the voice of the child him/herself:

> 'Much evidence will be gleaned from day to day interactions with children as practitioners build up their knowledge of what children know and can do, for assessment purposes and to inform future practice and provision. This evidence, often not formally recorded, provides the basis on which judgements are made and the focus of a moderation dialogue.'
>
> *Early Years Foundation Stage Profile Handbook 2013 (DFE, 2012)*

The revised documentation does give us some guidance on what that process might look like, and in general these are:

- children should be involved fully in their own assessments
- all adults who have significant interactions with the child in *should* be involved in the process
- systematic observations *must* be made in a wide range of contexts and day-to-day experiences
- planning *should* build on experience at home and in previous settings
- parents *must* be kept informed throughout the early years
- observations *must* be matched to the expectations of the early learning goals (and the 'Development Matters' statements)
- observations *should* be used to plan future learning experiences.

How practitioners do this is up to the setting to decide, using any guidance they care to seek, including that produced by Local Authorities, consultants and trainers, or commercial companies. The majority of settings now have well-established systems for incorporating observations, photographs and contributions from children and their families, and sharing these with everyone involved.

So, during the EYFS, there is a single legal requirement for assessment:

- 'Observe, and use your observations to help children make progress, and to make summary judgements at ages 2 and 5'.

---

2. The requirements for assessment at the end of the EYFS

These requirements can be found in The Early Years Foundation Stage Profile Handbook, which is reprinted every year. Practitioners should make sure they update their knowledge of this document, as there are changes (sometimes minor, sometimes major) every year. The document contains essential guidance on assessment, appropriate to all practitioners, not just those working in Reception classes,

The EYFS is now a statutory stage of the National Curriculum for England, and as such is bound by the same legislation as state (maintained) schools, including the requirement for a formal assessment at the end of the key stage.

'The EYFS Profile summarises and describes children's attainment at the end of the EYFS. It is based on ongoing observation and assessment in the three prime and four specific areas of learning, and the three learning characteristics.'

Early Years Foundation Stage Profile Handbook 2013 (Standards and Testing Agency; DFE; 2012)

So, at the end of the EYFS, the requirements are that practitioners must:

- within the year during which the child reaches the age of five, assess every child, using the EYFS Profile statements and the Characteristics of Effective Learning (taking into account the detailed requirements of this process).
- within the final term, provide a written report to parents, which includes the outcomes of the profile assessment and any other information which the setting wishes to include.
- provide copies of this assessment to parents, to the child's next teacher and local and national authorities.

The next chapter has detailed information about the two statutory assessment processes – the Two-Year-old Check, and the EYFS Profile.

3. The requirements for keeping individual and curriculum records during the EYFS, and reporting on these to parents

Settings are required to keep individual records for all children in the Foundation Stage. These should contain general, personal and curriculum information:

The Statutory Framework states that:

'Providers must maintain records and obtain and share information (with parents and carers, other professionals working with the child, and the police, social services and Ofsted as appropriate) to ensure the safe and efficient management of the setting, and to help ensure the needs of all children are met. Providers must enable a regular two-way flow of information with parents and/or carers, and between providers, if a child is attending more than one setting. If requested, providers should incorporate parents' and/or carers' comments into children's records.

Records must be easily accessible and available (with prior agreement from Ofsted, these may be kept securely off the premises). Confidential information and records about staff and children must be held securely and only accessible and available to those who have a right or professional need to see them. Providers must be aware of their responsibilities under the Data Protection Act (DPA) 1998 and where relevant the Freedom of Information Act 2000.'

Statutory Framework for the EYFS: (DfE; 2012)

Providers *must* allow parents access to see their child's records if they request it, and EYFS providers *must* give parents a written summary of a child's development and learning at 2 and 5 years. Parents should be involved in the assessment process on a regular, ongoing basis and encouraged to participate in their child's learning and development.

At the end of the Foundation Stage:

> 'All EYFS providers completing the EYFS Profile must give parents a written summary of their child's attainment using the 17 ELGs and a narrative on how a child demonstrates the three characteristics of effective learning.
>
> Year 1 teachers must be given a copy of the EYFS Profile report together with a narrative on how the child demonstrates the three characteristics of effective learning.
>
> Reports should be specific to the child, concise and informative. They may include details from ongoing assessment, links to age related bands in Development matters and details from any other assessments appropriate to the individual child in order to help to identify the appropriate next steps in learning.
>
> *Early Years Foundation Stage Profile Handbook 2013* (Standards and Testing Agency; DFE; 2012)

If a child leaves a setting at any time before the end of the Reception Year, their education record and a common transfer file must be sent to their new setting or school. The information in this file should include a copy of every report to parents alongside their ongoing curriculum record. The transfer information can be sent electronically or in paper copies.

So, during the EYFS, there is a legal requirement for every child to have a record, containing information unique to that child, including information on the child's development and learning, which reflects the seven areas of learning and development, the Characteristics of Effective Learning from the EYFS, and the developmental stages from Development Matters. The setting or school must report in writing in a summary of the child's recorded progress at two and five years old, and may report in writing at any other time. Copies of any written Reports to the child's parents must be contained in each child's record.

Exploding some myths

Should I be writing down everything I observe?
There is no requirement to write down everything, or even most, of what you observe during the Foundation Stage. It is up to you to decide what is significant, what to write down or record in other ways, and what to keep. It is important to discuss and agree with your colleagues how much evidence to collect, and what form it should take.

How much evidence should I keep?
It is up to you to decide how much you keep, but once you have recorded your judgements on the child's record, you do not need to keep all the evidence. It is important to discuss and agree with your colleagues how much evidence to keep after your regular transfer of information to children's records.

How much time must I spend on assessment?
There are no requirements on how much time you should spend on observing learning, the format your observations should take, or how often you should do them. There is some informal advice that you should spend 20% (about one day a week) in all sorts of observation, in order to have enough information to plan next steps.

What should our personal records look like?
The format for records is for the setting to decide, although there are some requirements on things it must contain. Records can be paper based or electronic. Some Local Authorities provide templates, but these are guidance.

Do I have to update 'official' individual records every half term?
There is no requirement to do this more than once a year, but most practitioners do update some sort of record about once a half term to help them to keep the curriculum on track, and to make sure individual children don't get missed. If your informal records can give you all this information, and if your manager agrees, you could follow the requirement and only update records once a year, but this would be unusual.

What should our reports to parents look like?
It is up to the setting to decide, although there are now some examples of formats

for the Two–Year–old Check (A Know How Check from NCB), and many others on line. The EYFS Handbook has a suggested format for an EYFS Profile, which could also serve as a Report to Parents. Many settings already report in writing every year and there are many formats available on the Internet to help you decide on your own.

Do we have to keep children's records forever after they leave? We have nowhere to store them!

No, there is some confusion about how long you should keep different sorts of records, but the accepted guidance is that you should keep curriculum records for three years. This is a reason for making them manageable, or consider secure electronic storage, but remember that CD/DVD storage isn't considered to be permanent, as there is a possibility that the information may become degraded or corrupted over time.

Further information about children in the Foundation Stage, including any changes, is contained within the Assessment and Reporting Requirements (ARA); Standards and Testing Agency document, which is published every year for practitioners in England.

Some guidance on record keeping

Here are six principles for record keeping (the written information resulting from assessment by observation). Each principle is followed by some points for discussion in your setting.

1 **Record keeping must be meaningful and have a purpose.**
   Have we discussed the purposes of our record keeping? Do we feel it makes a real contribution to children's learning, or is it just a chore?
2 **The task of keeping records must be manageable and sustainable.**
   Have we invented a time-greedy monster? Can we sustain the model we currently have?
3 **Records must capture the range of children's attainment, achievement and progress.**
   Do our records really celebrate the whole child or do they lean towards literacy and numeracy, allowing important areas of interest and learning to take second place (or no place at all)? Do we include all the areas of learning identified in our planning?

4 **Records will reflect the individuality of every child and the diversity of their backgrounds.**

   How much time do we spend finding out about the children as individuals, and where does this knowledge feature in what we say about them and how we value their learning and their culture?

5 **All significant participants in children's development and learning should contribute to the information-gathering.**

   Do we include contributions from colleagues – teaching assistants, nursery nurses, nursery officers and other professionals? Do we include parents and children in recognising and celebrating achievements as partners, not just as an audience for our judgements?

6 **Records should be shared with the child.**

   Do we genuinely share both assessment and record keeping with the children, making them partners in the learning process, understanding what they do well and what they need to do next? How do they contribute to the process?

Guidance in the rest of the UK

The other countries in the UK have also produced guidance on assessment and reporting to support their most recent versions of early years curriculum documentation.

   Universal access across the UK to pre-school education is a recent development for us all, and the four governments have responded in different ways, on different time-lines, and with differing emphases. Their guidance on assessment has a common theme of observation, their development of 'end-of-early-years' assessments has progressed at different rates, and in some of the countries in the UK such assessments are still in development. However, readers who work in other countries or other school systems may find the following information of interest in exploring the wider implications of recording and reporting children's achievements:

The Foundation Phase in Wales (age three to seven)

Foundation Phase requirements:

   In Wales, organization of year groups takes a different form, with a Foundation Phase running from 3-7 years, and a statutory teacher assessment at seven against goals for the whole Phase, has now been implemented. The Guidance on Statutory Requirements for teacher assessment at the end of the Foundation Phase (age three to seven) in Wales contain the following:

'Teachers are required to make their statutory teacher assessments at the end of the Foundation Phase (the year in which the child reaches seven years) against three of the Areas of Learning.

- Personal and Social Development, Well-being and Cultural Diversity.
- Language, literacy and Communication Skills.
- Mathematical Development.

(There is currently no statutory requirement at the end of Nursery, reception or year 1. However, leaders/headteachers, where appropriate should ensure that all practitioners gather evidence to inform each child's progress in all Areas of Learning.)

Statutory assessment arrangements for the end of Foundation Phase and Key Stages 2 and 3 (Welsh Government, February 2013)

The previous Guidance for practitioners in Wales on assessment in the Foundation Stage is helpful and clear, continues to be recommended, and contains the following:

'The information that has been collated should be used in future planning and to inform parents/carers of the children's progress.

Some information will be needed in the short term while some will need to be kept for the longer term. It is important that any form of recording is not burdensome for staff and that the amount of paper is kept to a minimum.

The type and range of record-keeping to assist with practitioner assessment is a matter for settings/schools to decide. Elaborate arrangements for recording and retaining evidence of assessments are neither required for Foundation Phase assessment purposes nor necessary to satisfy Estyn inspection requirements.'

(ESTYN is the Inspection system in Wales) Observing Children (DCELLS, 2008)

and:

'Teacher assessment covers the full range and scope of the Foundation Phase learning continuum. It should take account of evidence of achievement in a range of contexts, including that gained through discussion and observation throughout the Foundation Phase.

At the end of the Foundation Phase, teachers are required to assess and report outcomes attained by each child by means of teacher assessment in:

- Personal and Social Development, Well-Being and Cultural Diversity
- Language, Literacy and Communication Skills in English or Welsh
- Mathematical Development.'
    Framework for Children's Learning for 3 to 7-year-olds in Wales
    (DCELLS, 2008)

The Foundation Stage in Northern Ireland (age three to five)

In Northern Ireland, the preparation for implementation of Foundation Stage Assessment has been part of a whole curriculum revision, which integrates the Foundation Stage within the National curriculum for primary and secondary learning. The Non-statutory Guidance for the statutory assessment at seven includes the following references to observation and assessment – four useful contributions are included here:

'Assessment is an integral part of the learning and teaching process. By gathering information about a child's progress over a period of time, teachers build a comprehensive picture of the learning in order to plan future work. In developing Assessment for Learning practices in the Foundation Stage adults should, when appropriate, engage in dialogue with children about their learning.

Good planning and effective assessment are closely related. Since the purpose of teaching and the main purpose of assessment are to help children to learn, teaching and assessment need to be planned together as complementary aspects of the one activity. In turn, the information obtained from assessment should be used to inform the planning process.

In the Foundation Stage, you have flexibility to interpret the Areas of Learning to suit the needs, interests and abilities of your pupils. Effective assessment during this stage will ensure that:

- teaching builds on your pupils' current stages of development, their needs and interests, and previous experiences;
- your pupils are active participants in the assessment process;
- they are motivated and their learning is challenged;
- you have, and share, realistically high expectations of your pupils as learners;
- they can receive appropriate support; and
- there is a two-way flow of information with parents/carers.'

'Observation is a natural and essential part of effective assessment practice. Observations should take place throughout the day and in a range of contexts. Regular observations and written records of each pupil's development provide a comprehensive picture that will inform your planning and enable you to take account of individual needs. You may use your observations in both formative and summative assessment.

Observations also allow you to evaluate practice.

You can reflect on any aspects of provision where pupils have experienced difficulties, need more time or need additional resources/ opportunities. Information from the same observation can be useful for both assessment and evaluative purposes.'

'As part of its assessment policy and practice, your school should agree a flexible system for recording observations. This should reflect the principles and pedagogy of the Foundation Stage and each Key Stage. For example, you might record observations using pro formas, notes (post-its, sticky labels or notebooks), samples of pupils' work, photographs, DVD evidence and audio recordings. Features of best practice include:

- teacher and classroom assistant involvement;
- making planned and spontaneous observations;
- using positive language, focusing on what the pupil can do or does know;
- including the date and information that identifies the when, where and who, for example during play in the sand area John and Amy …
- describing what the pupil(s) did and, when appropriate, including quotes to document the pupil's language;
- using agreed abbreviations for the areas of the room, pupils' names etc. (if you find these helpful);
- keeping information factual, specific and brief; and
- including any follow-up action required.'

All from: *Learning, Teaching and Assessment in the Foundation Stage;*
Supporting Foundation Stage Teachers in Assessment and Reporting;
(CCEA, 2012)

The Curriculum for Excellence in Scotland (age three to sixteen)

The Curriculum in Scotland has also been reviewed in recent years, resulting in a range of integrated documents covering the whole age range. The approach to assessment is coherent across all stages, as these examples show:

'For monitoring and tracking to be successful, records of children's and young people's achievements and progress need to be manageable.

Staff should use assessment information from a wide range of sources to monitor learners' progress and plan next steps in learning. Assessment information should be shared and discussed with the learner, parents, other staff as appropriate, and partners involved in supporting learning. All can contribute at appropriate times to setting targets for learning and ensuring appropriate support for each child and young person.'
Curriculum for Excellence, Building the Curriculum 5: A Framework for Assessment (The Scottish Government, 2010)

and:

'From time to time teachers also take stock of their learners' progress and achievements in order to be able to plan ahead and to record and report on progress. This is vital in ensuring that learners' progress is on track and that action is being taken to address any problems at the earliest possible point.

This taking stock relates to broad standards and expectations, for example deciding whether a level for a curriculum area, or part of an area such as reading, has been achieved or what additional learning and support is needed.

It involves teachers in evaluating a range of evidence produced over a period of time to provide a summary of progress and achievement, including for qualifications and awards. It can be carried out in a number of ways, including by weighing up all relevant evidence, taking account of the breadth, challenge and application of learning.'
Curriculum for Excellence, Building the Curriculum 5: A Framework for Assessment (The Scottish Government, 2010)

Education legislation in any country or system will change over time, and you need to keep up with the changes that affect you. In England, and increasingly in the other countries in the UK, information is published annually which lays out the regulations and guidance on assessment, including any changes to legislation. It is vital to keep up with documentation such as this, because some legislation changes very quickly, and sometimes very quietly!

The Progress Check at age two, and the EYFS Profile

4

This chapter is mainly concerned with the details of the most recent changes to the early years curriculum in England, and in particular, a new assessment (the Progress Check at Two) and the revisions to the EYFS Profile for five year olds.

Following the revision of the Foundation Stage curriculum in 2012, there was a significant shift in the focus of the documents, and in the pressures for accountability. Although many settings were already in the habit of reporting annually in writing to parents, and managing observation as a central feature of assessment for learning, and to compiling Learning Journey documents for children, these professional practices were neither statutory nor universal. The Revised EYFS included a requirement for an annual report for every child, whatever their age, and added a formal check of progress during the year in which children have their second birthday.

Assessment and reports to parents must be based observations of children, and these observations must be made when children are following their interests and initiating their own activities. There is more emphasis on knowing the child, less emphasis on over-complex record keeping, and practitioners must observe *how* children learn (using the Criteria for Effective Learning) as well as *what* they learn (using the developmental checklists in Development Matters).

The revised Framework sets out clearly how these new assessment and reporting activities must be undertaken from 2012/2013, and they present some challenges to the profession:

- Coinciding with the government funding for expansion of early years provision for two year olds, practitioners working with some of the youngest children in the setting must now produce a short written review of each child's development *during the year following the child's second birthday*. This activity will focus the minds of many who have not previously been required to do this, and;
- A new, streamlined version of the Profile, used *'in the final term of the EYFS'*

will now require practitioners to look at complex statements of development through a 'best fit' model of assessment.

These changes will involve many practitioners and their managers in some hard thinking about how they organise their planning and their time, when and why they collect information, and how they present this in a way that parents and carers can understand.

Assessment in England – at a glance

Child's age	Age 0-1	Age 1-2	Age 2-3	Age 3-4	Age 4-5
Ongoing assessment		Observational Assessment			
		and 'Learning Journey' collections (no statutory format)			
Statutory assessment			Two Year old Check (between 24 & 36 months)		EYFS Profile (in the final term of the child's fifth year)
Records	Complete at least once a year	Complete at least once a year	Complete at least once a year	Complete at least once a year	Complete at least once a year and hand on to Y1
Reports to parents	Report to parents (verbally or in writing)	Report to parents (verbally or in writing)	Statutory written report to parents	Report to parents (verbally or in writing)	Statutory written report to parents
Information to local authority	No	No	No, but OFSTED will ask to see the information & discuss the process	No	Yes

The EYFS Progress check at age two

Why do we need a check when the child is two?

The reasons for this have been clearly and helpfully explained in the practitioner guidance provided by Hampshire County Council:

'The most rapid period of brain development is in the first three years of life when early experiences trigger the brain connections that will remain for life. In some crucial areas of development such as emotional control, response to stress, communication and language and sensory and physical development, a child needs to have the right experiences within sensitive periods when the brain is ready for this wiring to take place. The windows of sensitivity are strongest at this point in a child's life and putting support in place at this time will provide most benefit to the child's development.'

Guidance on completing the Two-Year-Old Check (Hampshire County Council, 2013)

Hampshire County Council also reflect on the research evidence which concludes that:

'1. After the age of three, it becomes much more difficult to make changes in both a child's development and in parental behaviour.
2. Mothers and fathers play the most important part in raising a child.'

Supporting Families in the Foundation Years; DFE/DH; 2011

This research also contributed to the construction of the Revised EYFS and resulted in the Two-Year-Old check of development, currently completed by the child's key person, in close collaboration with parents. The outcomes of this check are deemed to belong to the parents, and are not reported to the local authority or the DFE, although Ofsted inspectors will certainly be interested in looking at both the process and the outcomes as they inspect settings and schools.

In the Revised Framework for the EYFS (England), the Areas of Learning and Development are re-organised into *three Prime Areas* (Personal, Social and Emotional Development; Communication and Language; and Physical Development) and *four Specific Areas* (Literacy; Mathematics; Understanding the World; and Expressive Arts and Design). Another change is the addition of the Characteristics of Effective Learning (Playing and exploring – engagement; Active Learning – motivation; and Creating and thinking critically – thinking).

The EYFS Framework emphasises the importance of the Prime Areas of Learning and the Characteristics of Effective Learning when assessing children's progress at some point between 24 and 36 months.

The Revised Framework states that:

'When a child is aged between two and three, practitioners must review their progress, and provide parents and/or carers with a short written summary of their child's development in the prime areas. This progress check must identify the child's strengths, and any areas where the child's progress is less than expected. If there are significant emerging concerns, or an identified special educational need or disability, practitioners should develop a targeted plan to support the child's future learning and development involving other professionals (for example, the provider's Special Educational Needs Coordinator) as appropriate.

Beyond the prime areas, it is for practitioners to decide what the written summary should include, reflecting the development level and needs of the individual child. The summary must highlight: areas in which a child is progressing well; areas in which some additional support might be needed; and focus particularly on any areas where there is a concern that a child may have a developmental delay (which may indicate a special educational need or disability). It must describe the activities and strategies the provider intends to adopt to address any issues or concerns. If a child moves settings between the ages of two and three it is expected that the progress check would usually be undertaken by the setting where the child has spent most time.'

Statutory Framework for the EYFS; (DFE; 2012)

Shortly after the publication of the Revised Framework, the National Children's Bureau published guidance on the progress check (A Know How Guide; NCB 2012) and this clarified the principles and purposes of the progress check, alongside some non-statutory guidance and examples from settings. Many Local Authorities and support agencies have since produced models for what is now referred to as the Two-Year-Old Check, and many are available on line for practitioners who need guidance and ideas for formats.

The role of parents and carers in this process is full and significant. Parents/carers will be engaged in the following ways:

- Practitioners must agree with parents '…the most useful point' when the summary should be made. If possible, it should be provided in time to inform the work of Health Visitors in compiling the Healthy Child Programme health and development review
- Practitioners must give parents an opportunity to discuss the summary with them
- Practitioners must discuss ways in which the summary can be used to support the child's learning at home
- Practitioners should encourage parent/carers to share the information with other professionals (such as their health visitor or future nursery teacher) – providers/practitioners must have the consent of parents before sharing the information directly with other professionals.

Here are some tips for completing the Two-Year-Old Check:

1 Practitioners must inform parents that the Two-Year-Old Check is going to take place, and should discuss when the best time would be for this to happen. Practitioners must explain that the Check is in addition to the Healthy Child Progress Check completed by Health Visitors. (NB An integrated version of the two checks, led by the child's Health Visitor, is planned to start in 2015).

2 If the child is new to your setting, **the check should be completed after a six week settling in period, and as close to the child's second birthday as possible**. However, you may decide to delay the process if:

   a. you feel the child's attendance or the balance of full and part time placement limits your chance to get to know them well

   b. the child is only just two, or is new to your setting, and may need longer to settle in

   c. the child's individual or home circumstances give cause for concern.

   BUT don't delay, especially if you have real concerns about the child, or the child is approaching their third birthday.

3 The Progress Check should be completed by the child's Key Person, who will incorporate information from parents/carers and other professionals including (where appropriate) practitioners in the child's previous setting. The draft Progress Check should be checked by the manager or leader of the setting before copies are sent to the parents.

4 The Check should contain:

   a. *simple narrative statements about the child in the three Prime Areas and in the Characteristics of Effective Learning,* using the statements from Development Matters when making judgements

   b. *comments from the child* about what they like and can do (the voice of the child)

   c. *comments from parents/carers* and any other professionals who know or work with the child

   d. *indications of any concerns* about the child's development and learning – these should have already been discussed with parents, so they do not come as a surprise to them

   e. *indications of areas for development* in the future.

5 Parents should be given a copy of their child's Check, and an opportunity to discuss this with their child's Key Person.

6 A copy of the Check should be added to the child's record.

Any search engine will help you with information and examples of blank and completed formats – search for 'Two-Year-Old Check'.

Information on the combined assessment (the Healthy Child Progress Check, and the EYFS Progress Check at Two) will be issued at a later date.

> 'From September 2012 all providers must complete the progress check for two year olds. The long term goal is to implement an integrated Health and Education Review at aged two by 2015, in order to support greater partnership working between education and universal health services for the benefit of children and families.'
>
> *Progress Check at Age Two*; London Borough of Islington; 2012

The Revised Early Years Foundation Stage Profile

I accept that this section may be of less relevance to practitioners working in other countries within and outside the United Kingdom, but the latest guidance on pulling together all the assessment work done in children's early years has useful things to say to all of us.

In this section I will be referring to the following documents:

- *The Statutory Framework for the EYFS*; DFE, 2012
- *National Curriculum Assessments;* **Early Years Foundation Stage Profile Handbook;** *(DFE 2012)*
- **National Curriculum Assessments; Assessment and reporting arrangements (ARA) Early Years Foundation Stage 2013;** *(Standards and Testing Agency; DFE; 2012)*
- **Exemplifications 1-17, for each of the Early Learning Goals of the EYFS Profile;** *(Standards and Testing Agency; DFE; 2012)*

The EYFS Profile assessment was originally introduced in 2006/07 to replace baseline assessment in Year 1, and included the collection of information from observations across 119 statements (Early Learning Goals).

Since 2007, Profile outcomes have been included in annual written reports to parents, and information is given to the next teacher, who is expected to take account of the information when planning for Year 1.

Profile data has also been used to provide information on the progress of individuals, groups, cohorts, schools, and Local Authorities, and has been analysed to give further information on the performance of groups within both the local and the national cohort. This analysis has included examining and publishing the performance of boys/girls, children with SEN, children from ethnic groups and those from disadvantaged backgrounds.

From 2012, the Revised EYFS has been in place, and the revision of the curriculum has included a revision of the EYFS Profile.

What has NOT changed?

- The assessment still takes place no later than 30 June in the final term of the year when the child reaches their fifth birthday.
- The outcomes are reported to parents, included in the child's record, and reported to the Local Authority.
- The assessments are informed by the practitioner's observation of children mainly involved in child-initiated activities.
- The Profile should take account of contributions from the child, parents and other relevant adults.
- The single purpose, repeated in new guidance, is 'To provide a reliable, valid and accurate assessment of individual children at the end of the EYFS'.

What's different? (Unless otherwise stated, words in italics are from the EYFS Profile Handbook 2013)

- Assessment must be made against the Early Learning Goals (ELGs) *and* the three Characteristics of Learning (CEL) exemplified in the EYFS Framework.
- Although *the number of Early Learning Goals* has been dramatically reduced, many of the previous goals are embedded in the new statements. The 17 revised goals are written in short paragraphs, and '*Practitioners are asked to make a best fit judgement for each ELG. The Profile Handbook gives exemplifications for each ELG. The ELGs must be taken as whole statements, and should not be divided up for assessment. 'Best fit' does not mean that the child has equal mastery of all aspects of the ELG. Practitioners should look to the whole of each ELG description when making this summative judgement.*
- The assessment judgements now enable practitioners to acknowledge whether a child has exceeded or not yet attained each of the ELGs. *Practitioners should use the exemplification to inform their decisions as to whether a child*

has met the level of development expected at the end of the EYFS for each ELG, has exceeded that level or not yet reached it (emerging). The Handbook gives examples to amplify the 'exceeding' judgements, but does not give equivalent detail for the 'emerging' judgements. Practitioners are advised to use the statements from the Revised Development Matters to aid their decisions (Early Education; 2012).

- <u>The use of P scales</u> has been clarified. If a child has not yet reached some or all of the goals, Development Matters statements, NOT P scales, should be used to assess and report the stage of development of the child in each of the appropriate ELGs. *P scales are an assessment tool designed for use at Key Stage 1 and should not be used for assessing children in the EYFS... in these instances practitioners should refer to the Development matters guidance.*

- <u>The Characteristics of Effective Learning</u> are seen as central to a child's learning, and *vital elements of support for the transition process to Year 1.* They underpin all the areas of learning and describe *processes rather than outcomes.* The commentary on the characteristics *should consist of a short description (one or two paragraphs) of how the child demonstrates the three characteristics of effective learning – playing and exploring; active learning, and creating and thinking critically.*

- The use of information from the Profile to ease <u>Transition to Key Stage 1 (Year 1)</u> is emphasised. *The transition between the EYFS and Year 1 should be seamless... It is important that Year 1 builds on the successful principles and approach encapsulated in the EYFS.* The Profile Handbook expands the information in the Statutory Framework, emphasising the importance of allocating time for EYFS practitioners and Y1 teachers to discuss each child's Profile, not just the outcomes of the 17 ELGs, but the Learning Characteristic narratives.

- <u>Using the Profile in Key Stage 1.</u> There is a new emphasis on the continuity of provision between the EYFS and Key Stage One, not just in taking note of the assessment made by practitioners, but incorporating the information so the curriculum provided in Year 1 is appropriate to the individuals in each class or group, as they move between the two stages of education. *Beyond the 20 items of the EYFS profile, practitioners may provide any additional information needed to enable Year 1 teachers to plan an effective curriculum and provision for all children. Decisions about this additional information should be made by each setting and reflect the characteristics and requirements of that setting. This will enable the Year 1 teacher to have a fully rounded picture of the attainment of each child in order to plan the curriculum. Year 1 teachers should be involved in*

EYFS Profile moderation in order for them to understand the judgements made by Early Years practitioners.

- The language of assessment in the EYFS Profile has been clarified. Helpful amplifications, explanations, examples and glossaries have been compiled to help practitioners, parents and managers in their discussions of the process of observational assessment, and to clarify points where misunderstandings might occur and suggested *lines of enquiry* to be followed when completing assessments against the Characteristics of Learning. For example, within the Principles for the EYFS Profile assessment, there are helpful explanations of key vocabulary used in the Handbook, which have been condensed here:

  o **Observational assessment** –
    - involves reaching an understanding of children's learning by watching, listening and interacting
    - may be planned, but some observations may be a spontaneous capture of an important moment
    - of everyday activities will provide evidence in more than one area of learning
    - does not require prolonged breaks from interaction with children, nor excessive written recording.

  o **Responsible pedagogy** –
    - enables each child to demonstrate learning in the fullest sense
    - takes place in a range of contexts
    - requires a rich learning environment
    - respects each child as an individual
    - values children's efforts, interests and purposes
    - high quality adult interaction
    - results in an accurate, reliable and consistence assessment of children's learning which will inform planning for Year 1.

  o **Child initiated activity** –
    - reflects the first Characteristic of Effective Learning (Playing), and depends on observing learning which children have initiated rather than only focusing on what they do when prompted.

  o **Embedded learning and secure development** –
    - is demonstrated without the need for overt adult support
    - is observed when children initiate the use of skills and abilities that they have learned themselves.

- o **Links in the areas of learning** –
  - are often interlinked, and may also link to the Characteristics of Learning
  - will mean that observations can be effective in covering more than one area at a time.
- o **Practitioner knowledge** –
  - of the child will offer the majority of information for the Profile
  - may need to be amplified in adult-led activities to offer additional insight
  - will be used to glean information from day to day interactions with children
  - is often not always formally recorded, but provides the basis for judgements and for moderation.
- o **Contributions to the assessments** –
  - should involve the children
  - require two-way flow between settings and home.
  - should build on the insights of adults who have significant interactions with the child.
- Exemplifications. The Standards and Testing Agency has produced a full set of exemplifications (one document for each of the 17 ELGs). These are collections of examples from settings and schools of activities, which has been observed and sometimes recorded by children, practitioners and parents. The full set of exemplifications can be downloaded from: http://www.education.gov.uk/schools/teachingandlearning/assessment/eyfs/b00217443/eyfs-exemplification
- Internal Moderation of the profile assessments is carried out in settings/schools, and local authorities are responsible for 'providing a robust moderation process' and this is described in detail in the EYFS Profile Handbook. Moderators should expect that *the majority of evidence will come from the practitioner's knowledge of the child and observations of the child's self-initiated activities (Moderators must not scrutinise recorded evidence without the practitioner present).*
- The uses of the EYFS Profile data are now much more explicit, particularly the clear expectation that Teachers in Year 1 will use the information to plan an appropriate curriculum, and that data will be used to *monitor changes in levels of children's development and their readiness for the next phase of their education.*

The primary uses of EYFS Profile data are:

o To inform parents about their child's development against the ELGs and the characteristics of their learning.

o To support a smooth transition to Key Stage 1 by informing the professional dialogue between EYFS and Key Stage 1 teachers.

o To help Year 1 teachers plan an effective, responsive and appropriate curriculum that will meet the needs of all children.

• Good Level of Development (GLD) and Profile scores. During the period when data was collected on the old Profile format, this was used by the government, Ofsted, local authorities and schools to establish whether schools and individual children were attaining a 'good level of development' (GLD). It is no longer possible to use this measure, so at the time of writing, the following information has been published by the DFE:

'From 2013 children will be defined as having reached a GLD at the end of the EYFS if they achieve at least the expected level in:

o The Early Learning Goals in the prime areas of learning (Personal, Social and Emotional Development; Physical Development; and Communication and Language) and;

o The Early Learning Goals in the specific areas of Mathematics and Literacy.

Point Scores:

The average point score across all Early Learning Goals:

• Emerging =1
• Expected =2
• *Exceeding =3*

o This would measure the total number of points achieved on the EYFSP

o The national measure would be the average of every child's total point score

o http://www.education.gov.uk/schools/teachingandlearning/assessment/eyfs/a00224219/eyfs-2013_2

Sadly there is no mention, nor seemingly any intention of including the Characteristics of Effective Learning in this measure.

What are things I must do? Remember, the words 'must' and 'required' mean the law! – (*Again, unless otherwise stated, words in italics are from the EYFS Profile Handbook 2013*)

- Ongoing observational assessment. *During the final year of the EYFS, practitioners must undertake ongoing (formative) assessment to support each child's learning and development.* (NB There is NO requirement that this is recorded in any specific manner or at any specific points in time)
- Summative assessment. In the final term of the EYFS *practitioners must review their knowledge of each child using information from all sources to make a judgement for each ELG.* Using the exemplification material, all their evidence, and considering the entirety of each ELG, *Practitioners must make a judgement for each ELG as to whether the child's learning and development is best described by:*
    - the description of the level of development expected at the end of the EYFS (expected);
    - not yet at the level of development expected at the end of the EYFS (emerging); or
    - beyond the level of development expected at the end of the EYFS (exceeding).
- The Characteristics of Effective Learning. Short descriptive paragraphs describing how the child demonstrates these must be included in the Profile assessment. *These descriptions must reflect ongoing observation of the child within formative assessment processes and should take account of all relevant records held by the setting and include information from the child, their parents and other relevant adults.*
- Children for whom English is not their home language. *The ELGs for Communication and Language and Literacy must be assessed in relation to the child's competency in English.* However, the remaining ELGs may be assessed in the context of any language, including English.
- The needs of individual children are highlighted in the Revised Framework. Practitioners are required to take individual needs into account when making judgements. *For instance, there may be children who are at an earlier stage of development than others in the cohort; some may have summer birthdays. These children and others may be highly active and more likely to demonstrate what they know, understand and can do in situations which are sympathetic to this inclination, often outdoors.* At last there is now a requirement to be sensitive to

the needs of individual children, including boys and children who learn better out of doors!

- Reporting the Profile assessment. *All EYFS providers completing the EYFS Profile must give parents a written summary of their child's attainment using the 17 ELGs and a narrative on how a child demonstrates the three characteristics of effective learning. Year 1 teachers must be given a copy of the EYFS Profile report together with a narrative on how the child demonstrates the three characteristics of effective learning. All EYFS providers must report EYFS Profile data (the 17 ELGs) to their local authority for each child, upon request.* (NB there is no requirement to report to local authorities on the Characteristics of learning!)

- Keeping records. Settings and schools *must* keep a record for each child, which includes the information listed in the EYFS Framework, and a copy of the Two Year Old Check and the report on the EYFS Profile. These records must be updated at least once a year. *Providers must maintain records and obtain and share information (with parents and carers, other professionals working with the child, and the police, social services and Ofsted as appropriate) to ensure the safe and efficient management of the setting, and to help ensure the needs of all children are met. EYFS Statutory Framework: 2012*

- Academies and Free Schools must also meet the statutory requirements if they receive Government Grant for children in the EYFS (details in the Assessment and Reporting Arrangements; ARA for the current year).

Now the regulations are out of the way, we can continue to explore how to assess in a way that is helpful to learning, and how to create and keep manageable records.

Assessment methods: the good, the bad and the plain pointless! 5

Assessment for learning is like cooking: it is great to have lots of recipes, but some become favourites, and can become so familiar that we can cook them without thinking, and without asking ourselves whether they are 'fit for purpose'. Every so often, just like a chef, we need to refresh our memories about other ingredients and recipes.

This chapter is intended as a resource for you and your colleagues, a collection of assessment methods for you to dip into as you work. There are many different ways to assess learning, and I have tried to include as much of the whole range as I can, although any collection will inevitably have gaps.

When you are selecting methods of assessment, it's vital to keep the principles in mind, and particularly those associated with the following:

- Is it *reliable*? – Can I really count on the information? Does it really show me what the child can do?
- Does it give *useful* information? – will the information be in a form that I can use? Will we use it?
- Is it '*time efficient*'? – is the information gathered by this method worth the time invested in doing it? Have we planned enough time to do it?

Here are some of the methods we have at our disposal, with their advantages and disadvantages. If you need more ideas about how your assessments can be recorded, see page 96, where the range of ways of recording is explored.

Observation methods

Observation (informal or participant observations)

All humans use informal observation to make hundreds of assessments of other people every day. Parents, practitioners and teachers use these informal observations to assess how well children are developing. The information often enters our memory without conscious effort, and informs our opinion of the person we observe and what they can do.

> Observation
> Reaching an understanding of children's learning by watching, listening to, and interacting with children as they engage in activities and experiences and demonstrate their specific knowledge, skills and understanding.
> *EYFS Profile Handbook 2013; Standards and Testing Agency*

Advantages

Informal observation just happens, it's like osmosis, and happens often without the observer being conscious of what they are doing or seeing. These observations build gradually into a complex picture of the child, most of which is not written down.

Disadvantages

This sort of observation is random, and the picture of the child may be skewed because of this. In a class or group, some children may not be observed as much as others, or may be observed over a narrow range of activities, times of day or locations.

Observation (formal)

These observations are built into the day or the week. They can be long or short, but they have a clear focus. This focus may be a single child, a group, or 'focus' children. The observation could also be of an activity or skill, an area of learning, or a particular place. The focus can be 'loose' or 'tight', with room for manoeuvre if the focus or activity changes or develops. Planned observations are usually recorded in writing, photo sequences or other recordings.

Advantages

Practitioners find planned observations useful in ensuring that they observe every child over a range of activities throughout the year, and that the curriculum provision is systematically covered.

Disadvantages

Once a focus has been decided, it can be difficult to accept children's own agendas, or to register additional information that is not related to the original focus.

Comparative narrative

A comparative narrative can be a written account of two children of the same age at the same time, or of the same child on two different occasions. It is often used to monitor the development of children with additional needs. You could also use this method to quickly assess whether two children are making the sort of progress you expect. In these observations, it is particularly important not to compare the children with each other, just with objective criteria.

Advantages
Observing two children at once can be a more efficient use of time. Observing one child on more than one occasion and comparing the things you find out will make your assessments more reliable.

Disadvantages
It is easy to get distracted watching one child and not give equal time to the other, possibly missing important elements of their learning. It's also difficult to keep your view objective and keep your focus on a manageable number of clear criteria.

Assessment task

Assessment tasks are activities planned by the adult, and usually carried out in adult-directed situations, often in small groups. The tasks may be formal, with concrete outcomes, such as models, pictures or writing/mark-making, or informal, with a specific challenge set for the children. The activity is observed by the adult who keeps a record of what happens.

Advantages
The systematic nature of this sort of assessment gives it an element of standardisation where children can be compared to each other and to national, local or school/setting/cohort norms. It can reduce the variables associated with more informal observation.

Disadvantages
Assessment tasks can be rigid and formal, relying on outcomes rather than process. Because the same activity is often used across a group or class, it may lack relevance to individual children's interests and they may not perform as well as they could in an activity they choose themselves.

Tick sheet or checklist

These assessments are often used as a quick check in a group of children on a single criterion (colour/number/letter recognition, handedness, pencil grip) or single activities and skills (can cut along a line, can dress and undress unaided, can build a tower of three bricks). Sometimes these are recorded during adult-directed activities. At other times they are completed during free play or other activities where the children are using the focus skills.

Advantages
They are quick and easy to record.

Disadvantages
They can only be used with clear 'yes/no' answers, and only show evidence at a single moment in time.

Snapshot observation

This is a quick and useful way of monitoring what is going on, what an individual child is doing or how children are using of the different areas of the setting. If you make regular snapshot observations, they can help you to see which children regularly use the area or activity, those who never do, and how friendship groups are developing. The observer makes notes of who is doing what, whether any children are 'drifting' and any area that is overcrowded or under-used.

Advantages
Snapshot notes are useful when evaluating whether your organisation and activities are meeting the needs of the children.

Disadvantages
One snapshot isn't useful in itself, you need to do this sort of check regularly, and *use* the information to confirm the success of your environment, organisation or planning or to change it.

Tracking

Tracking is a method of following a child, an activity or even a group over time to find out more about what happens. It can also be used to track participation in a particular activity, for example, the writing or block area, or to look at gender involvement. The observer usually decides on a timescale (perhaps every five minutes over a session or even a day) when they will look up from what they are doing and log what the focus child is doing/who is involved in the activity and so on. The record can be made on a plan of the room, by logging the path or track of the child, or in brief notes of what the observer sees. The information can be presented in a time chart, a pie graph or just as a 'trail' on a plan of the room or setting.

Advantages
This assessment can be done alongside other activities, and the observed child is less likely to be aware of the observer. The observation can also give you information over a longer period of time and space.

Disadvantages
The observer needs to be well organised and have a reliable watch or timer! It is easy to forget to look at the right intervals and this may make the observation useless!

Timed sampling

Timed sampling is similar to tracking, but in this method the observer watches the child or children for a set time (one, two or more minutes), then makes notes of what happened during the time, watches for another set period and writes again. The observation can take anything from a few separate minutes to half an hour or more, and can be done in a block or at different times during the day.

Advantages
The observer can watch without trying to write at the same time. This often results in better information as the observer does not miss things when they are writing.

Disadvantages
There are no obvious disadvantages to this method of observation, and many early years experts recommend it, particularly for inexperienced practitioners and those who find it difficult to watch and write at the same time.

ABC – reflective event sampling

This method is often used when a child is having problems managing their behaviour. The letters ABC stand for Antecedent (what happened before the event), Behaviour (the tantrum, outburst or other worrying behaviour) and C the Consequence (what followed the event or behaviour). The observations happen every time the behaviour happens to see if there is a pattern or trigger to the problem behaviour. The record continues over sessions, days, or a week, to see if a pattern appears. The records are analysed to help with behaviour management.

Advantages
ABC offers a way of doing systematic monitoring of the possible triggers in difficult behaviour. This makes it much easier to see patterns, for instance, the trigger may be a particular child, a new situation or even an energy dip just before snack time.

Disadvantages
This sort of systematic observation can be difficult to maintain, particularly when the child is already taking up a lot of your time. It's important to involve everyone, to have a simple way of recording in three columns – A, B and C and to keep the sheets somewhere handy!

Baseline

Baseline assessments are often made when children start at a setting or school, or when they move from group to group. The assessment usually consists of a series of statements, often with yes/no answers. They are sometimes used while discussing the child with their parents or carers or during home or pre-entry visits. Some settings complete these baseline assessments by observing the children during the first weeks in the setting or when the children have had time to settle in.

Advantages
Baseline assessments done through observation in the setting and conversations with parents can be a useful way of monitoring progress at later points in the child's time in the setting, or when they leave.

Disadvantages
Baselines can produce unreliable information, as they are assessments at a critical stage in a child's life, when they may be under huge stress. Some parents see baseline assessments as a test of their parenting, and they may answer in the way they think shows them, and their child, in the best light!

Observation diaries

Some settings make the writing of regular diaries a part of every Key Person's job. This means observing, writing notes, making comments, and taking photos of any other significant events and behaviours for each of the children in their key group. Children with additional needs often have a daily diary, which goes with them from setting to home and back, and parents make comments as well as practitioners.

Advantages

This sort of continuous assessment of progress and learning is a very good way of following a child's progress and is particularly useful in recognising individual interests and in personalising learning. Parents often really like this sort of anecdotal recording, and some settings encourage parents to contribute too.

Disadvantages

Diaries take commitment. Parents love to have regular feedback on what their children are doing. Make sure you don't start on this sort of assessment record unless you can keep it up!

Sociogram

A sociogram is a pictorial or diagrammatic map of the contacts and friendships a child makes during a day or over a period of time. The child's name is in the middle of a page, and directional arrows link them with children who approach them, or who they approach in play. These are best done during free play sessions or child-initiated activities.

Advantages

Social relationships are very important to young children. Recording these over time gives another dimension to your knowledge of the children. It is also a relatively easy way to record information.

Disadvantages

Some very sociable children may spend long periods on their own. Young children make and break friendships very frequently.

Questioning of individuals and small groups

This sort of assessment is often used in plenary sessions, and some practitioners focus on a small group of children each day to get coverage of the whole group and more information about individuals' learning.

'The two main styles of questioning are:
Closed questions, which tend to have a specific focus and usually only allow for one correct answer. Closed questions are useful in:

- ascertaining what children have understood; for example, in a story
- encouraging less-confident children to provide short answers
- acting as a stimulus/springboard for the introduction to extended conversation.

Open questions which tend to be short (sometimes just one word; for example, 'who?', 'when?', 'why?') and provide children with the opportunity to think and discuss a number of possibilities, solutions and ways forward.'

Observing children (DCELLS, 2008)

Advantages (open questions)

Open questions give children the opportunity to think and discuss a number of possibilities, solutions and ways forward. They also allow for an individual response to an activity idea or object.

Disadvantages (open questions)

They are time consuming, and some practitioners find open questions difficult to think of, as most questions they used in the past may have been closed.

Advantages (closed questions)

These tend to have a specific focus and usually only allow for one correct answer. They do have a place as long as we are aware of them. They can be helpful in finding out what children have understood; for example, in a story, in encouraging less confident children to provide short answers, or acting as a stimulus for the introduction to a longer conversation.

Disadvantages (closed questions)

They do not usually allow for deep thinking on the part of the child.

Longer forms of assessment incorporated in records

Portfolio or learning journey

This is a collection of annotated and dated evidence of the learning and development of one child (photos, comments, observations, pictures and other creations). This portfolio is collected over time, sometimes several years, and is used to celebrate achievements and to provide information for parents and particularly to the next setting or school. Some settings include *all* their assessment information in this folder or file, and see it as the single collection of evidence for each child. Some settings and schools are now collecting information and presenting it digitally in e-portfolios, PowerPoint presentations and other computer based collections.

> 'The Learning Journey is a continuous journey through which children build on all the things they have already experienced and come across new and interesting challenges. Every child's learning journey takes a personal path based on their own individual interests, experiences and the curriculum on offer.'
> *Principles into Practice Card 3.2 Enabling Environments: Supporting Every Child The Early Years Foundation Stage pack* (DCSF, 2008)

Advantages
When children are involved in the selection and annotation this is one of the best ways of celebrating the whole child, recognising their individuality and valuing what matters to them.

Disadvantages
The process can be time consuming and some profiles can become very full. This can make the process too cumbersome for transfer, so weeding out and reducing the number of items is important. Electronic collections must be backed up!

Photographs, tape and DVD recordings

Most settings now use photographs to expand their collections of assessment evidence. Some settings also use DVD, video and dictaphone or tape to record children's achievements.

Advantages

Photos and DVD give a good insight into children's learning and make the learning much more visible. They bring real colour to individual experiences and are a reminder to practitioners of what happened.

Disadvantages

This sort of assessment is only useful if it is annotated or transcribed and dated. This can be extremely time consuming.

Case studies

A case study is an in-depth observation of one child over time. It is also a way to collect information about a child who is a cause for concern, or who may have additional needs. Case studies are often undertaken by students, or those in further training, to improve their understanding of child development.

Advantages

Case studies are great for collecting in-depth information about individual children.

Disadvantages

They are time consuming to collect, read and interpret.

Nationally moderated assessment methods

National, age-related assessments

The EYFS Profile and teacher assessment by level at the end of Key Stage 1 are examples of national, age related 'teacher' assessments. In the early years, these assessments are administered by the practitioners in the school or setting, and are used at set points in the school year. They sometimes acknowledge the child's age, and they are used for all sorts of purposes, including measuring the success of teaching. The results are often used out of context and they sometimes take no account of starting points or 'added value' from baselines.

Some independent school systems have evolved their own age-related assessments. The High/Scope series of assessments is an example of this work (see www. highscope.org).

Advantages

They use standard, age-related criteria for whole cohorts, and have detailed guidance on how they should be used. The outcomes can be used to gain information about standards across the school, the local area and the country, and performance of different gender, ethnic or cultural groups.

Disadvantages

Variations in the ways practitioners understand and look for the criteria as they make their judgements can affect the reliability of the findings. Moderation meetings and visits are vital in helping practitioners to make good judgements and come to agreements about evidence.

Tests

Diagnostic tests

These tests are often used when a child is being assessed to diagnose a learning difficulty. They are standardised (the scores are established by using them in very large groups of children) and they usually focus on a narrow band of skills or aptitudes. Some diagnostic tests can only be administered by educational psychologists, therapists, or other staff with responsibility for special needs, because these people have specialist skills, impartiality and training in administering, marking and interpreting the results of the tests. They are also knowledgeable in advising on next steps in learning, or strategies for support.

These tests are often administered outside the classroom or setting to preserve the neutral conditions required. Diagnostic tests are also used to establish the needs of gifted children, or to move forward in the process of preparing a statement of special needs.

Advantages

These tests are very specific, and give detailed information to help with diagnosis and support for learning difficulties or gifts. The impartiality of the person administering the test enables them to see the child objectively, something that their practitioner, teacher or key person may find more difficult.

Disadvantages

Tests of this sort only cover small parts of the curriculum, usually those that are the most easily tested or observed. Some practitioners have reservations about testing by a stranger, or outside the secure area of the classroom or setting.

Standardised attainment/achievement tests

These tests measure knowledge and/or skills and are administered in tightly controlled situations. Because they have been standardised over large numbers of children, they can be used to produce a statistical profile in comparison with a national or age-related norm. Reading and maths tests, IQ tests and Key Stage SATs are examples of standardised tests.

The outcomes of these tests have been used to produce statistical information, but this is not always robust because the variables are so wide across practitioner judgements, children and settings or schools.

Advantages

These tests are easy to administer, providing the child can understand the questions! If properly constructed, standardised and marked, they give reliable information and statistics.

Disadvantages

Tests of this sort only cover small parts of the curriculum, usually those that are easily tested or observed. If the curriculum is inappropriately geared to the test, not the programmes of study or the whole curriculum, then children get a limited experience and can be put at a disadvantage in later years. Children who excel in areas of learning that are not easily tested, such as social relationships or the arts can be disadvantaged by these tests.

> 'Standardized tests can't measure initiative, creativity, imagination, conceptual thinking, curiosity, effort, irony, judgment, commitment, nuance, good will, ethical reflection, or a host of other valuable dispositions and attributes. What they can measure and count are isolated skills, specific facts and function, content knowledge, the least interesting and least significant aspects of learning.'
>
> *Bill Ayers, University of Illinois*

Challenges

A few challenges for you – which types of assessment would be appropriate for the following situations?

- To find out why a child in your group has tantrums.
- To find out if the role-play area is well used by both boys and girls.
- To find out if you should spend money on left-handed scissors.
- To find out where a particular child spends his/her time during child-initiated play.
- To find out whether a child in your group has a hearing problem.

So – you can choose! Of the methods described above, some will be familiar to you, others less so. The advantage of knowing what you *could* do, is that you have a whole range of assessment tools in your toolkit, and can make informed choices about how and when to use them – new ingredients for a new flavour of assessment.

Now on with recording!

From observation to records

6

This chapter is divided into two sections:

- Recording assessment for learning (AfL) – a continuous process, undertaken daily and weekly.
- Regular record keeping against agreed national or local standards – a periodic process, undertaken at intervals of about six to eight weeks.

Summing up this evidence and making judgements and writing down the things we find out, sifting out the important information, and recording it at regular intervals, is the next stage in our journey through assessment. Many settings and schools have agreed ways of recording ongoing assessments, and formats for recording children's achievements and developmental progress, others are still looking for the holy grail of the most time effective way of recording the huge amount of information we collect about each child. This chapter explores some of the different ways you could

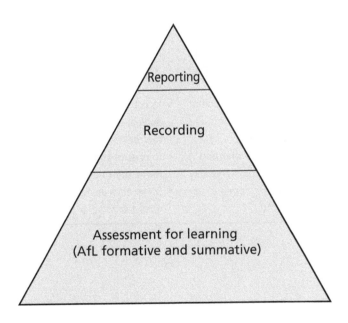

consider when recording your initial and ongoing observations of children's achievements and developmental progress.

Some of this information is part of the AfL processes, noting what you see as you see it. However, everyone needs to pause at regular intervals and look at what the information from AfL is telling us. These processes are collectively described as 'summative assessment' – summing up what we know so far, and recording the significant bits, often with some reference to national guidance, stages of development, or goals. The point at which 'formative assessment' (AfL) becomes 'summative assessment' is here – where assessment becomes recording.

What is the difference between formative and summative assessment in the early years?

Formative assessment is a process used by practitioners and teachers:	Summative assessment is a process used by practitioners and teachers:
• to **collect relevant evidence** of children's progress and achievements, mainly through observation of children in activities which they have initiated themselves	• to **sum up information and assessments** at agreed intervals (usually at between six to eight weeks or half a term)
• to **register and note significant achievements or difficulties**, not all of which is written down	• to take stock and **select key evidence** from AfL on which they can make judgements
• to ensure that they observe and assess **every child** in their group or class	• to **assess progress against agreed outcomes or targets**, using common statements and indicators, usually from an agreed curriculum,
• to provide immediate **feedback** on learning to children, their parents and to colleagues	• to **condense information** by selecting significant pieces of evidence and incorporating these in manageable records
• to include and value **contributions from all the adults** in the setting, and in the child's family	• to **record** individual progress, on trackers, records or other documents
• to **inform planning** and next step, ensuring that future planning and target setting **improves teaching and learning**	• to **communicate information** to a range of audiences, including parents and the children themselves
• to ensure that **observations are planned regularly**, and do not just happen randomly.	• to **ensure that the curriculum continues to meet the needs of the children**.
• Formative assessment is often referred to as 'Assessment for Learning' (AfL).	• Summative assessment is often referred to as record keeping or tracking.

Formative assessment

Formative assessment almost always takes place in the setting when the children are present. It involves us in collecting evidence of various sorts, and it is important to remember that not all of this evidence will be written down.

> 'Ongoing assessment (also known as formative assessment) is an integral part of the learning and development process. It involves practitioners observing children to understand their level of achievement, interests and learning styles, and to then shape learning experiences for each child reflecting those observations.
>
> In their interactions with children, practitioners should respond to their own day-to-day observations about children's progress, and observations that parents and carers share.
>
> Assessment should not entail prolonged breaks from interaction with children, nor require excessive paperwork. Paperwork should be limited to that which is absolutely necessary to promote children's successful learning and development.'
>
> *Statutory Framework for the EYFS; DFE; 2012*

Formative assessment in the early years is almost entirely done through observation, although small amounts of evidence can be usefully collected during adult-led sessions or by other assessment means. In England, the guidance on percentages suggests that 80 per cent of evidence should be collected during chidinitiated activities and a maximum of 20 per cent during adult-led or adult-initiated activities.

Summative assessment

Summative assessment involves us in sifting through all the evidence from formative assessment, including the evidence that has not been written down, and deciding what it is telling us about the child. Summative assessment almost always involves writing or recording our judgements, often on an agreed record, common across the setting, the school or even the local area. These are usually referred to as curriculum trackers or curriculum records.

> 'When a child is aged between two and three, practitioners must review their progress, and provide parents and/or carers with a short written summary of their child's development in the prime areas.

In the final term of the year in which the child reaches age five...the EYFS profile must be completed. The Profile must reflect ongoing observation; all relevant records held by the setting; discussion with parents and carers, and any other adults whom the teacher, parent or carer judges can offer a useful contribution.'

Statutory Framework for the EYFS; DFE; 2012

The process of linking formative and summative assessment, and considering the evidence you have collected goes a bit like this:

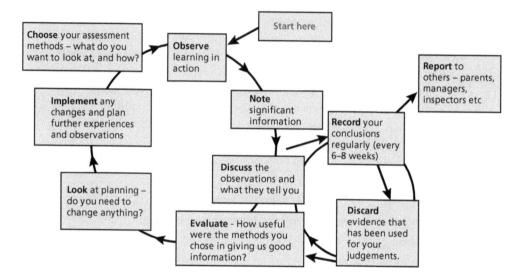

Making less from more – the art of condensing information

Whenever we decide to write something down, we inevitably condense it. Imagine writing down every single thing you see when you are observing a child, and imagine how long it would take to read! Even when we write a simple sticky note, or make a tick on a sheet, we are condensing our judgements of what we see and know about the child and writing the important bits.

At regular intervals we need to take all the 'already condensed' information in our AfL bag for each child and see what the collection is telling us. At this point we usually make an overall 'summative' judgement, and record this on a schedule, tracker or profile, often using agreed statements to help with our decisions. In England, practitioners and teachers use the Development Matters statements and Early Learning Goals; in Wales and in Northern Ireland, the Pre-school Outcomes and the Key Skills statements in the Foundation Phase; and in Scotland, the Curriculum Areas in the Curriculum for Excellence and the agreed outcomes of this.

The diagram below attempts to describe how the English curriculum for the early years is condensed into a summative assessment of readiness for school, the EYFS Profile. At the end of the EYFS, 514 Development Matters statements are condensed into 115 Early Learning Goals, which are then condensed into 104 EYFS Profile statements plus 13 additional statements, which register attainment beyond the goals.

How do the curriculum and assessment fit together? In England it's like this:

The Curriculum content (<u>what</u> children will be learning)

The curriculum areas	The aspects	The Development statements (from Development Matters)	The Early Learning Goals (ELGs)	The 'exceeding' descriptors (from the Profile Handbook)
Curriculum planning, observational (formative) assessment and summative assessment at 24-36 months			Summative assessment at five – the Profile	
Prime Areas				
Communication & Language	Listening & attention	Development statements for each area, divided into the aspects, cover 6 overlapping stages of development: • birth-11 months • 8–20 months • 16--26 months • 22–36 months • 30–50 months • 40–60+ months These statements are used to assess children throughout the Foundation Stage, and to identify children who are at one of the **'emerging'** levels of development.	1 goal	1 additional descriptor
	Understanding		1 goal	
	Speaking		1 goal	
Physical development	Moving & handling		1 goal	
	Health & self-care		1 goal	1 additional descriptor
Personal, social & emotional development	Self-confidence & self-awareness		1 goal	
	Managing feelings & behaviour		1 goal	1 additional descriptor
	Making relationships		1 goal	
Specific Areas				
Literacy	Reading		1 goal	1 additional descriptor
	Writing		1 goal	
Mathematics	Numbers		1 goal	1 additional descriptor
	Shape, space & measures		1 goal	
Understanding the world	People& communities		1 goal	1 additional descriptor
	The world		1 goal	
	Technology		1 goal	
Expressive arts & design	Exploring & using media & materials		1 goal	1 additional descriptor
	Being imaginative		1 goal	
TOTAL 7 Areas	17 sub-divisions		17 goals	17 additional descriptors

The Characteristics of Effective Learning (<u>how</u> children will be learning)

The Characteristics of Effective Learning		Detailed characteristics in Development Matters	Possible lines of enquiry when completing the Profile commentary
Playing & exploring – engagement	Finding out and exploring	12 additional statements	Explanatory text and 3 lines of enquiry
	Playing with what they know		Explanatory text and 3 lines of enquiry
	Being willing to 'have a go'		Explanatory text and 3 lines of enquiry
Active learning – motivation	Being involved and concentrating	10 additional statements	Explanatory text and 2 lines of enquiry
	Keeping trying		Explanatory text and 4 lines of enquiry
	Enjoying achieving what they set out to do		Explanatory text and 2 lines of enquiry
Creating and thinking critically	Having their own ideas	11 additional statements	Explanatory text and 3 lines of enquiry
	Making links		Explanatory text and 3 lines of enquiry

Although the revisions to the curriculum have reduced both the complexity of the curriculum structure and the number of goals, there is still a danger that the richness of the curriculum and the complexity of children's interests and achievements, may be lost in the simple reporting of seventeen goals. As the revised curriculum is implemented and assessed it becomes ever more important to give space, time and weight to *how* children learn, observing and reporting on the Characteristics of Effective Learning.

Learning is not a tidy thing, and observing learning is an art, not a science. Practitioners need many tools in their observational toolbox, and here are some of the many ways that you could observe children as they work and play. They are not in any particular order, except that they move from the least formal and time consuming to methods, which need a real commitment of time and energy. They are followed by a selection of processes for condensing the information you have observed into summative assessments.

Some methods for recording AfL

Of course, we need to preface this section with a reminder that *not all observations are written down!* The latest guidance says that:

> 'Observational assessment involves reaching an understanding of children's learning by watching, listening and interacting as they engage in everyday activities, events and experiences, and demonstrate their specific knowledge, skills and understanding.
>
> It is the most reliable way of building up an accurate picture of children's development and learning, especially where the attainment demonstrated is not dependent on overt adult support. Observational assessment is key to understanding what children really know and can do.
>
> Some observations will be planned but some may be a spontaneous capture of an important moment. It is likely that observations of everyday activities will provide evidence of attainment in more than one area of learning.
>
> Observational assessment does not require prolonged breaks from interaction with children, nor excessive written recording. It is likely to be interwoven with high quality interactions or conversations in words or sign language with children about their activities and current interests.'
>
> *EYFS Profile Handbook 2013; Standards and Testing Agency*

Some of the most useful information you collect about young children is collected almost unconsciously, like osmosis, soaking into your brain and memory through your eyes, ears and even your skin, enriching your knowledge of the child, and supporting your other judgements. However, it is very risky to rely on this method alone. It is not systematic or reliable enough without planned observations and some note-making systems that ensure coverage of the curriculum and all the children.

Watching

The guidance practitioners have now encourages watching. Of course, you are not just watching in a neutral way, you are watching through your 'professional glasses' – looking for information about the child or children you are with, and if you are experienced, you may be able to watch and be involved with the activity at the same time. Don't underestimate the difficulty of just watching! It takes nerves of steel to watch without accidentally leading or dominating the activity, but it will give you a wealth of information, and of course, you may decide to jot down a few important words after you have watched an activity – but don't feel that you must. You can also watch at times when you are not leading an activity – watching children getting dressed to go outside, during snack and meal times, or when a colleague is telling a story or singing. Watching for one minute or five, indoors or outside, with one child or the whole group, will give you the confidence to make those 'holistic', whole child assessments of what individuals can do and enjoy. Watching is an extremely useful activity in itself, and we should all do it more often.

Advantages

This method is excellent for getting to know individuals in your group. It is also very subtle, and the children will have no idea that you are observing, so they won't be tempted to perform for you. It's also quick and efficient – you can just watch at any time, while you are leading an activity, or not. Jottings may result, but mostly they won't, and this method is about increasing the knowledge of individuals that you carry in your head.

Disadvantages

It's always difficult to make time for just watching, so you need to agree with your colleagues and your manager that watching is an important part of the day and week. It's also dangerous to think you can do all your observations by just watching – there is some information that needs to be collected more systematically and some that should be recorded.

Sticky notes or computer labels

This is a very common method, popular with practitioners. All the adults carry packs or sheets of these notes or labels with them as they work. They jot down informal observations of children's achievements as they work, collecting these as they go. Some settings and schools overprint sheets of computer labels with simple systems for circling areas of learning and so on as well as leaving space for information about individuals. Pads or sheets of these can also be left in a number of places around the setting/classroom and in outdoor areas for ease of use. Once completed, they are transferred to individual records or files. They are used in a similar way to notebooks.

Advantages

This method is good for jottings and odd notes. They can be easily transferred to individual files without re-writing. It is great for recording what parents say, and for using as you work, or as you watch (see above).

Disadvantages

Some practitioners and teachers make this simple method into a chore by copying out all their notes again, rather than sticking the notes into children's records or onto index cards (see below). Sticky notes can prove expensive, but computer labels (although more cumbersome) are cheaper. Another disadvantage is that notes can get lost. They are not useful for longer observations.

Photographs

Digital and ordinary photographs are now routinely used to record children's achievements and progress. These are more useful if they are dated and annotated. Filing the photos in a digital folder for each child on the computer is one way of keeping track without having to print them all.

Advantages

This is an excellent way of capturing the moment, and children can get involved by taking photos of their own work and achievements, and recognising the efforts of others.

Disadvantages

Colour printing can be expensive. If you take a lot of photos, sorting and annotating them can be time consuming. It's worth getting cameras that automatically date the photos.

Other technology

Video and audio tapes, and dictaphones can be used to record children's achievements and progress.

Advantages

These technologies are excellent for capturing the activities of children with additional needs, speech and language difficulties or mobility problems. They are also a useful tool for tracking progress over time in language, reading or social behaviour. Children enjoy using dictaphones to record their own activities.

Disadvantages

Audio tape recordings need to be transcribed if they are to be useful. These methods can be expensive in equipment and your time.

Tablet computers and android phones such as iPhones and IPads

Some settings and schools are using tablet computers and phones to make observations of children in the EYFS, and they say they find these an excellent way of catching learning with photos and notes. Software firms are now producing programmes linked to the revised EYFS, and particularly to the EYFS Profile. For example, http://mrandrewsonline.blogspot.co.uk/2012/07/ipadsipods-as-observation-tool-in-eyfs.html has a blog contribution from a practitioner in a school where iPad tablets are used with a specially produced EYFS Profile observation programme.

Advantages

This appears to be a quick and efficient way of recording and organising information, making best use of electronic systems.

Disadvantages

Expensive to set up! You also need to be sure you keep this electronic information safe and have the necessary permissions from parents.

Index cards or postcards

These can be used to record children's individual developmental progress and achievements. Each child has a named index card, and these are used for informal jottings, logging other observations and making notes on activities such as paired reading. Some practitioners/teachers identify focus children for a day or a week by moving their cards to the front of the pile, and rotating these each week, so they focus on getting information about every child over half a term.

Advantages

This is a good, systematic way of ensuring that every child becomes the focus of your observations.

Disadvantages

This method should be used in conjunction with other methods such as observations, sticky notes and other ongoing records. If you *only* use this method, you may miss some important things because you are only looking at the focus child or children. In a big group it can take a long time to get through all the children if you only focus on one child at a time, hence the practice of identifying four or six focus children each week.

Notebooks or clipboards

Small notebooks are strategically placed in the setting or classroom both indoors and outside, where all practitioners have access to them as they work. They use the books to jot down their observations of significant achievements and/or important events or incidents that may have occurred, naming individual children where appropriate.

Advantages
Notebooks are a great way for collecting jottings in an easily available format. They are accessible to all staff, and need little time to use.

Disadvantages
You need to develop a system to make sure these notes are not just left unread in the books or a potentially useful assessment will not be used! You may need to transfer the notes to individual files or records, or vital information may be lost and this can be a time-consuming activity. A possible way round this is to read all the notebooks at regular staff meetings, so key staff can hear what has been said about their key children, making notes if necessary.

'Tick' sheets

Tick sheets, with children's names and spaces for a tick are often used for recording a simple skill achieved, an activity completed or a stage of development. Examples are 'Can recognise numbers from 1-5'; 'Can sit unsupported on the floor', 'Can put on and fasten their own coat' or 'Has had a turn at cooking this half term'. These sheets are sometimes used over longer periods of time to record growing skills and aptitudes. In some settings, children are involved in completing the sheets which indicate involvement in particular activities such as cooking or ICT.

Advantages
Tick sheets are quick and simple to devise and complete. These sheets can help you

to keep track of development and access to a range of activities or experiences, and several can be in use at the same time. Children can be involved in the recording.

Disadvantages
Tick sheets only record very simple information with little 'colour' to the judgement. Sometimes children can do a thing one day and not the next, or in one context and not another!

Observation sheets devised in the setting

Some settings agree on a format for recording observations. These often have pre-printed sections for recording names, dates, curriculum focus and so on. There are also spaces for recording the identified focus of the observation.

Advantages
These sheets are good for collecting systematic information, as you can make your own or personalise a blank for a specific activity or purpose.

Disadvantages
If you ONLY use these sheets, you could be missing things that are not on the list! They should be one of the tools, not the only one. A format for shorter observations and jottings should also be available.

Portfolios, learning journeys or records of achievement

Portfolios, more recently referred to as learning journeys are collections of children's work, photos, notes, observations and other information. Portfolios can include all the assessment information about one child, and they can be 'closed' (only accessible to adults and to parents on request), or 'open' (with the child fully involved in the collection and disposal of the contents).

Advantages
This method is very good for recognising the whole child and their progress across all aspects and interests. Most children love being involved. Information is all in one place for reporting to parents and getting an overview of the child. If they are 'rationalised' regularly by removing out of date or less useful contents, they can prove very informative at points of transfer.

Disadvantages

They can be time consuming to compile, particularly when children are involved. They also need to be weeded out regularly so the collection doesn't become too cumbersome. Everything should be dated, so a date stamp would be useful. Loose-leaf versions can become very untidy!

Methods of recording against national criteria: summative half-termly assessments

Paper-based tracking sheets – 'home grown'

Many schools and some early years settings have devised their own ways of keeping assessment records on paper. These follow the curriculum framework and practitioners tick, shade, highlight or otherwise indicate when statements, goals or levels are achieved. Some settings devise one simple sheet that covers all the goals or outcomes, and this is used alongside the curriculum guidance. This is very useful as an overview of the whole child across the whole curriculum.

Advantages

Tracking sheets on paper are more accessible for updating and interpretation than ICT based sheets, and this often makes it easier to involve others. The sheets are also easier to use when talking to parents or colleagues.

Disadvantages

Sometimes these trackers cover several sheets for each child, making them a bit cumbersome to use and interpret. Some settings devise complex 'keys' to indicate partial or less confident achievements – these are only useful if everyone understands what they mean!

Paper-based tracking sheets 'commercially' or locally produced

Some local authorities produce versions of these trackers for schools and settings to use, and others are available from publishers.

Advantages

Someone else has done the work, and as long as they fit your purpose, these can be great time-savers.

Disadvantages

Systems that have been devised outside your setting are often less successful than ones you have devised yourself, so you need to be sure you need an exterior model. In some cases practitioners do these external models, but also keep on with their own personal version, making double the work for themselves!

Condensed records of curriculum outcomes

Some local authorities, publishers and other suppliers, such as private nursery chains produce condensed versions of trackers for schools and settings to use. These provide overviews, some on a single sheet, with a key to indicate the relevant statements.

Advantages

Someone else has done the work, and as long as they fit your purpose, the single sheet versions could be very useful.

Disadvantages

The cost can be an issue, some may be more complex than you need, and if you need a reference document to learn how to complete and understand it, there could be a temptation to fill them in on 'autopilot'!

Computer-based (electronic) systems – 'home grown'

Many schools and some early years settings have devised their own ways of keeping assessment records on computers. These vary from simple overviews of progress to complex e-portfolios containing photos, scans of children's work, practitioner notes and contributions from parents and the children themselves.

Advantages

These personalised e-portfolios can be a fantastic way of involving everyone in recording progress, recognising achievements over a period and including children's individual interests. If you have devised a system that works for you, you are more likely to put the time into making it work.

Disadvantages

These systems can be time consuming, even if they children do some of it themselves. This method really appeals to practitioners who like ICT!

Computer-based (electronic) systems – commercially devised

Some computer-based systems are produced by commercial publishers and provider chains, and they allow practitioners and their managers to track progress against the EYFS and National Curriculum frameworks. Some also provide a range of ways of presenting information in charts and reports, which should enable practitioners to track children's development. Some also offer a tool to enable reporting to parents.

Advantages
There is quick retrieval of information in text and chart forms, particularly for evaluation and management purposes. Information can be produced in 'report to parents' format.

Disadvantages
This system needs dedicated time at regular intervals to transfer information from practitioner notes and so on. There is no space for photos. Reports to parents could seem a bit impersonal. Some systems need additional software, and cost may be an issue for some settings.

Methods of recording against national criteria: summative and end of stage assessments

Paper based systems – nationally devised

The Revised EYFS has placed great importance on informing parents about their child's progress. There are many example formats for both the Two Year old Check and the EYFS Profile, either on-line or in the Guidance.

The Know How Guide (NCB; 2012) includes a range of example formats for the Two Year Check, and local authorities are producing alternatives, many of which are available on-line.

The Profile Handbook offers a simple proforma for the revised Profile, including the 17 goals and the narrative for the Characteristics of Effective Learning (an editable format is available to download from http://www.lancsngfl.ac.uk/curriculum/assessment).

There is no requirement to submit data for the Two Year old Check, it is up to the setting to decide which format to use.

Schools and settings where the Profile is used are required to submit Profile data to their local authority electronically, either electronically, using agreed systems, including Excel, or on paper, using a printed version of the document. Local authorities are required to submit collated, authority wide data to the government, currently using COLLECT, a secure data system.

Advantages
Some smaller settings and schools will still prefer to use a paper version, so it is useful to have this alternative. However, more and more settings and schools will wish to use electronic systems, where support staff can input the data, saving valuable time for practitioners.

Disadvantages
Of course, when most schools and settings are using an electronic version, there may be some pressure to conform!

Computer-based (electronic) systems – nationally devised

As described above, the EYFS Profile in England is an 'end of stage' assessment, and its purpose is to summarise a huge amount of learning (over four or five years if you include pre-school and home experience) into a judgement on 'readiness' for the primary school curriculum. In England, this assessment condenses attainment into 17 statements. It has also been suggested by OFSTED that the Profile assessment in England should focus on a smaller number of outcomes, in order to enable Key Stage 1 teachers to maximize the progress that children make, closing the gap between advantaged children and those from less advantaged backgrounds:

> 'In addition, these good schools focus their baseline assessments sharply on the key skills needed by young children to engage in learning. Their assessments emphasise a core of communication, language and literacy. The assessments are straightforward and carefully moderated to ensure accuracy. The schools use their assessments to track children's progress right through to the end of Key Stage 1.
>
> The EYFS Profile, by comparison, is too broad an assessment and does not link effectively to subsequent Key Stage assessments. It provides a weak basis for accountability.'
>
> *Sir Michael Wilshaw, HMCI, Ofsted; June 2013*

Other versions, such as the E-Profile, are available to download from government departments, local authorities or to buy from publishers and other early years providers. They allow practitioners and their managers to track progress against the Development Matters statements towards the Early Learning Goals, and provide a range of ways of presenting information in charts and reports. Many, including the e-Profile also offer a tool to enable reporting to parents.

Advantages

The profile provides a quick way of retrieving information across the whole curriculum for individual children, groups and cohorts. The information is often available in text and chart forms, particularly for evaluation and management purposes. Information can also be produced in 'report to parents' format. Comparisons across classes, groups, schools and local authorities are easy to see, and national averages are displayed alongside school and local results.

The government now places great importance on the sharing of the Profile outcomes with Year 1 teachers, as well as with parents. This is particularly important for children who may not be ready for the more formal learning that often follows early years experience.

Disadvantages

These computer-based profiles are highly condensed and are of little use for planning or observation. Their role is to summarise learning at the end of the year. They need dedicated time at regular intervals for the transfer of information from practitioner notes and so on. There is a danger that if the practitioner uses summative assessments too early in the final year of early learning, their planning and observation may be restricted to the statements in the profile, not the wider bank of statements from Development Matters. However, the new requirement to report on the quality of learning as well as achievement in the seven areas of learning and development will help practitioners to practice on the abilities and interests of individuals, rather than reducing their experience to numbers.

Managing the evidence!

Once you have made your judgements and recorded them, you *don't* need to keep all the evidence! Some practitioners are worried about discarding evidence on which they have made their judgements, in case someone challenges them. However there is really no need to keep skip-loads of evidence just in case. If you have made your judgements honestly and professionally, there is no need to keep every post-it note, every photo or every piece of work done by every child, and there is even less need to send all of this on to the child's next teacher. The proper place for evidence that you no longer need is with the child, so send it home, unless the family already has a copy. Most children and their parents love to have their work.

This will leave a small collection of evidence, which will be much more useful to a new teacher or school. Most teachers would say that between three and five pieces of work, well chosen by you, or by you and the child together, will be much more helpful to them than a big collection. These pieces of evidence, together with the commentary on the characteristics of learning, and evidence of the child's interests and abilities, dated and annotated if necessary will ensure a good start to Key Stage 1.

Of course, selecting work for transfer is a time-consuming job, but if you plan time for it and do it with the children, it gives you a really good insight into what is important to the child, and how they want to be seen by their new teacher or practitioner. If you keep digital profiles with photos and other evidence in each child's folder on your computer (see below), these can be put on disc for parents and for the next teacher or school. Digital profiles are a very cost effective way of keeping evidence, they take up very little space and can be accessed by the children.

Using assessment and records to help with planning next steps is a thread through this whole book. How we go about this delicate task is the focus for the next chapter.

What does planning for assessment look like?

7

Much of the guidance on assessment in the early years advises practitioners to 'use their observations to inform planning'. This is easy to say, but less easy to put into practice, so in this chapter I will be exploring how schools and settings can genuinely attempt this complex job. This is not the place for examples of planners or formats for planning which take into account the outcomes of assessment. The best planners are those that practitioners develop themselves, sometimes referring to guidance or the work of other settings, and regularly reviewing both the process of planning and the documentation used to record it. It is, however, possible to set out the *process* of planning for assessment, to offer some underlying principles for this, and to give examples of the process in action.

In the guidance for the Foundation Phase in Northern Ireland, written in 2006, but still very relevant today, there is a helpful description of the different layers of planning for the curriculum in the early years, and this will be familiar to most early years practitioners:

> 'Long-term plans set out, in broad terms, the learning for a whole group of children, usually over a period of a year.
>
> Medium-term plans bridge the gap between the broad outline of the long-term plan and the day-to-day detail of the short-term plan. Medium term plans may refer to half-termly or monthly periods.
>
> Short-term plans should take account of the children's individual needs and be responsive to their ideas and spontaneous play. There should be enough detail to inform teachers and classroom assistants on a daily basis to ensure that the best use is being made of time, space and resources. These plans are likely to take account of recent observations and assessments of children.'
>
> *Understanding the Foundation Stage* (CCEA, 2006)

Most early years practitioners plan in this three-layered way, although their documentation may look different in its layout, content and quantity.

How do we make sure that there is time for assessment?

The only way to do this is to write it in your planning! It is vital to plan enough time for assessment at each of the layers of planning, because if we don't, this could happen:

> 'Practitioners must consider the individual needs, interests, and stage of development of each child in their care, and must use this information to plan a challenging and enjoyable experience for each child in all of the areas of learning and development.'
>
> *Statutory Framework for the EYFS*; DfE 2012

In 'Ten tips for assessment' (see page 00) I suggest that 20 per cent of the time you spend with the children should be used for assessment. This rather scary amount of time will, of course, cover *all* the assessments you do when the children are there, including:

- 'eavesdropping' and 'covertly watching' what children are doing, particularly in their play
- observing children through informal and planned observation activities and
- identifying the characteristics of effective learning
- tracking children and activities
- taking photos and other recordings
- talking with children as they play and work, asking and answering questions
- collecting and organizing concrete evidence such as photos and copies of children's work
- listening to children as they talk, read, sing
- talking with parents about their children's achievements
- working with children to collect and select items for portfolios
- listening to children as they report back on their learning during group and plenary sessions
- explaining to children what you are finding out and writing about their learning.

There are, of course, other assessment activities that must be fitted in around your time with the children, need to be planned into practitioners' work during the day, week and year. These include:

- contributing to informal discussions in the setting
- arranging and attending meetings to discuss planning and assessment
- attending training sessions
- getting involved in moderation of work in your setting and with practitioners from other settings
- sampling your evidence
- writing records and reports
- reporting to parents, managers and others
- analysing the results of your assessments.

If you start to count up the amount of time you spend on assessment, you will be amazed at how much you are doing, how often you are doing more than one of these things at a time, or how often you are making assessments as you do other things! Of course, this collection of assessment techniques can't be allowed to just happen. Many of them take dedicated time, and there is never enough time when you are working in education. So planning for assessment needs to be consciously built in at every layer of planning. If you are unsure about any of the terminology used in this chapter, refer to page 00 for more information on assessment techniques, and see the Ten Tips for assessment on page 00.

Stop feeling guilty!

One of the most important things when planning for assessment is to stop feeling guilty! The fact that you are reading this book indicates that you know the vital role of assessment in and for learning, but some practitioners will still feel guilty when they think they are 'just watching children'. Some will also be less confident in writing observations, 'catching the moment' in photos, or asking open questions to get good information from children. These practitioners need support as they improve their confidence and their assessment techniques.

> 'Ongoing assessment (also known as formative assessment) is an integral part of the learning and development process. It involves practitioners observing children to understand their level of achievement, interests and learning styles, and to then shape learning experiences for each child reflecting those observations.'
> *Framework for the EYFS;* DfE; 2012

The managers and team leaders in every setting must make clear that planning time for observation, and using the resulting evidence are two of the most important tasks for practitioners. Managers must expect to see observation in action when they visit groups of children. They must include assessment practice in the range of targets for improvement for individuals and the setting as a whole. They must see training for assessment as a real reason for meetings and training sessions both on-site and further afield. And most important, they must expect to see time and staffing allocated to assessment activities in long, medium and short-term planning.

Planning should not just be an activity with its own life, going forward on a sort of 'autopilot', which could result in activities and opportunities that do not meet the needs of any of the children. What we all need to do is plan flexibly, ready to change things as we begin to observe the planning in action, adjusting to what we see and what the children do. Of course, the first place that change will be needed is in short-term plans, the plans for the day and the week. These need to adjust to our daily observations, often to those we don't write down!

The best attitude to short-term planning is to plan in detail for the first day or two of the week, leaving the rest of the week in outline, and filling it up as the days develop, and children's needs emerge. This may mean some fairly dramatic adjustments and even abandoning something we have planned carefully on Sunday afternoon!

Planning needs to take into account the results of all your assessments, observations and other information. The different layers of planning will need to be adjusted in different ways, following different assessment methods, specifically chosen to give particular information.

What should short-term planning include?

Your short-term planning should be influenced by the notes and jottings you make in your daily work – sticky notes, notepads, photos, including the observations you don't even write down. It will be particularly responsive to what you see in child-initiated play activities, where the interests of individuals and small groups of children become evident; where you might pick up a lead for a new activity or centre of interest; identify the need for additional resources or see something that needs to be practised or reinforced. Adjusting your short-term planning is a daily possibility, as you ask yourself these questions:

- What have I seen today that may affect what I plan for tomorrow?
- Have any of the children asked for anything that I could provide?

- Have I seen any emerging interests that I could promote tomorrow by planning activities, reading stories or introducing new resources?
- When I watch the children in independent activities, are they able to use the skills I am teaching them in adult-led sessions, or do I need to adjust the content of my group times?

To fulfill these professional expectations, your **short-term plans** might include time for some of the following assessment techniques:

- **Build assessment into your written planners** for the day and the week. How are you going to identify time and space for observation? Once you have identified the time when the planned observations will happen, how will everyone know who you are going to look at and what you are looking for
- **Make sure there is always at least one person concentrating on observation during child-initiated sessions.** This time can involve you all in participant observations, don't try to do group work during these sessions!

'Each area of learning and development must be implemented through planned, purposeful play and through a mix of adult-led and child-initiated activity. Play is essential for chidlren's development, building their confidence as they learn to explore, to think about problems, and to relate to others. Children learn by leading their own play, and by taking part in play which is guided by adults.'
Framework for the EYFS; DfE; 2012

- Provide **plenty of jotters, sticky notes, stickers and simple observation sheets** around the setting, indoors and outside, so you can jot down significant information. Set up a simple way of organising these jottings so they are easily managed and accessible for discussions.
- **Leave time at the end of each adult-led session to quickly record the significant things that happened** – were all the children engaged? Did any child find this activity too difficult or too easy? Did any child surprise me, amaze me, worry me or puzzle me? This can be done on a simple sheet with the children's names listed. Remember, don't write about everything, just jot down the significant things.
- **Use cameras** to capture the moment. Digital cameras give you instant access to the things you see, so you can look at today's photos on the camera or a computer during your planned discussions.

- Plan to have **two adults present some of the time at group times**, one leading the session, the other observing all the children, or children who are the current focus.

- **Use Key Person groupings** as the organisation for small group times, so the person who knows these children best is able to observe their own group.

- **Set up a system for identifying 'focus children'.** This could be a file card index or other simple system to ensure you cover and revisit all the children regularly.

- **Plan some time for longer observations** when you can look at individual children more closely. Remember the guidance, and don't make these observations too long. It's better to plan more short observations than long ones that just put pressure on everyone:

- Discuss whether you could **build in some simple tracking** of activities or individuals to make sure you know what is happening in different activities or areas of the room or outdoor area.

- Make some sheets of **tips for assessing play** in different areas of your provision, listing some of the things you are looking for. Put these up in the areas of provision and the tips will remind you of what you are looking for in child-initiated play.

- **Make time at the end of the session or the day** to look at your observations and share them in the team. Have your short-term plan available too, so you can make adjustments on the spot.

- **If you are worried about an individual child**, plan some observations over a week, so you can collect information from different observers and in different activities. Remember:

'Some observations will be planned but some may be a spontaneous capture of an important moment. It is likely that observations of everyday activities will provide evidence of attainment in more than one area of learning.'

Assessment and Recording Arrangements 2013 (ARA) (Standards and Testing Agency, 2012)

What should medium-term planning include?

Your medium-term planning should be influenced by your regular record keeping. Every six to eight weeks, when you review your latest units of work, topics and skills development, recording the outcomes on children's curriculum records, you will reflect on whether your medium-term plans are meeting the needs of the children. You will be using the children's curriculum records to track progress towards the targets and goals you have set, and using the process to think about the curriculum for individuals and groups within your class. Adjusting your medium-term planning is a possibility every half term, by asking questions such as:

- Are we going too fast or too slowly through the curriculum?
- Are we managing to provide that ideal balance of security and challenge that really does scaffold children's learning?
- Are we meeting the needs of this particular group?
- Are any children getting left behind?
- Do any children need more challenge?
- Is the balance of child-initiated and adult-led activity about right for the children?

Your **medium-term planning** should include time for some of the following assessment techniques:

- **Plan some meeting and discussion time to look at these:**
  - o **The records of individual children and groups to see if there are any patterns across different records.**
  - o **Coverage** – did you actually cover everything you planned?
  - o Your planning and record keeping **process**, is it manageable and useful? Does it help you to manage the week and the half term?
  - o The guidance on curriculum and assessment to see how well you are **covering the curriculum.**
  - o A sample of children's **portfolios** to see if you have the right amount and range of assessment evidence.
  - o The previous half term's **topic** or centre of interest. Did it go well? Were the children interested? What did they learn?

- In the plan for the next half term, build in:
  - ○ Some **tracking** of activities and use of areas.
  - ○ **Time to talk with the children** about what they know, can do and are interested in.
  - ○ Time to **go through portfolios** to make sure they are manageable and well organised.
  - ○ Any **adjustments to the planning and recording process** that you have decided to make.

What should long-term planning include?

Your long-term planning should be influenced by your annual review of the curriculum, looking at how you manage the development of learning through a mixture of methods – the range of themes and topics; continuous and enhanced provision for child-initiated learning; the condition, use and access to resources and the way you help children to make progress in skills development. You will be using end-of-year assessments, such as annual reports, transfer records, and formal assessments, such as the EYFS Profile in Reception. Adjusting your long-term planning is a possibility every year. You will consider this at the end of the year as you reflect on the past year and the current group of children and ask: *Were the children engaged with the topics and themes we introduced, or should we consider revising the topic cycle to incorporate more of the children's own interests?*

- Do our records and reports reveal any gaps in children's learning?
- Did we miss anything vital?
- Did the children develop in the way we expected?
- Is there any way we can adjust next year's planning so it is more effective?
- Do we need any additional resources, or have we got resources that we are not using?

At the beginning of the new academic year, you will also look at your new group or class and consider whether your long-term plan is likely to meet the needs of the new group, as no two classes or groups of children are the same. Some questions might be:

- What is the gender balance of this group?
- Is this a young class, with the majority of children born in the spring and summer months?

- Will the cultural or ethnic balance of this group indicate different interests, language levels, social development?
- Are the children coming into my group straight from home, and what will this mean for my planning?
- How will our evaluation of last year affect next year?

Your **long-term planning** should include time during, and particularly at the end of the year for some of the following activities:

- Plan some meeting and discussion time to look at and discuss:
  - any **data** resulting from end-of-year records and assessments to locate any trends and gaps
  - information about the year and the group, resulting from writing **annual reports and records** and discussing these with parents and children
  - **your annual (long-term) plan** for the curriculum
  - your **cycle of topics, centres of interest** or themes
  - any information about **resources** you need to add, replace, reorganise or repair.
- In the plan for the next year, build in:
  - further **tracking** of activities and use of resources
  - time for **discussion** of assessment in informal sessions and more formal meetings
  - any **modifications you want to make to the planning and assessment** process at all three levels
  - any decisions you have made on **curriculum coverage, organisation and balance** of activities, such as your topic cycle or session plans
  - a point at the end of the year when you will discuss how well the year has gone.

And to conclude this section, here are some examples from practice:

- **Four practitioners** are tracking the way children access resources and are able to take them to the area of the setting that they choose. This gives them information about the organisation and layout of the resources, and will affect planning for the whole setting at long-term level.
- **Information from the EYFS Profile** is analysed by Maura and her teaching assistant. They find that the children in the current group, particularly the

boys, have low scores in fine motor control and using small tools. They look at their medium-term plan and how they could improve opportunities and resources for more fine motor activities, particularly during child choice times and in the outdoor area. They add some smaller tools and equipment to water play, mark making and the 'making area'. They also teach children how to use the tools in adult-led activities. During the rest of the year they monitor the use of these tools and add more as the boys become better at using them. The increased opportunity to use tools improves the skills of all the children in the group.

- **Danny observes a group of girls** in the role-play area. They are trying to make some clothes for a baby doll. They are using paper and are disappointed in their own efforts when the paper clothes fall off the baby. Danny offers some easy-to-cut fabric and fabric glue to make the job easier. The girls get very involved in this activity, but their scissor skills are not very good, and they need a lot of help. Danny adjusts his short-term plan again to plan some small group activities with scissors to improve the scissor skills of all the children.

- **The teachers in Reception** plan a topic about the seaside as part of their long-term topic cycle. They prepare a medium-term plan and then talk with the children about what they already know about the seaside. During this session they find that the majority of the children have never been to the seaside. The teachers postpone the topic until they find out whether they could take the children to the seaside before they embark on this part of their long-term plan.

- **At the end of the afternoon, two boys find a blue shopping bag** at the bottom of the brick box. They start to play a simple shopping game and are very disappointed when packing-up time is announced. The teaching assistant in the group observes this play, and suggests that they should adjusts the plan for the next day to include setting up a small role-play shop where she leaves the blue shopping basket. The following day she finds the two boys and tells them what she has provided. One of the boys is very excited and immediately gets involved in the shop play, where two other children join him.

- **Jodie and Mina are discussing the records of their key groups** of children. They note that there is no information for some children on whether they can 'sing songs, make music and experiment with ways of changing them' – one of the Early Learning Goals for Expressive Arts and Design. They plan to make this a focus for observation. They provide some nursery rhyme tapes and books for the book corner, and include more singing in group times, offering children the opportunity to perform a song to the group if they want to. Many do, and love doing it. Jodie and Mina get lots of information about singing, they find out that children are singing everywhere – outside, on the bikes, in doll play in the home corner, in the book corner – as well as during small group times.

- **Sammy is one of the focus children** for observation in his pre-school group. During the week, the adults notice his interest in books, and particularly non-fiction books about animals. They plan a visit to the library for the following week, inviting parents to come too. Sammy's mum joins the library with Sammy and the librarian offers to come to the pre-school to read stories once a week. To Sammy's delight she asks him if he would like her to bring some animal stories. The adults decide to include regular visits to the library in their medium-term plans.

- **Bernice is a childminder** who looks after her own small baby and Sandy (aged three and an only child). When they visit the local child-minding group Bernice notices that Sandy stays very close to her and will not join the other children in their play, becoming distressed when Bernice encourages her to join in. Bernice talks to Sandy's parents and they decide that Sandy needs more opportunities to meet and play with other children, before she starts school. Bernice contacts another childminder and arranges to share activities with her on a regular basis, planning joint visits and meeting in each other's homes. By the time Sandy goes to school, at four, she is much more comfortable playing with other children, although she still sometimes needs support.

These examples give some idea of the many ways that practitioners adjust their planning in response to what they observe, asking questions and examining their practice.

Of course, reviewing and asking questions often results in change to planning. However, we should remember that asking the questions does not always result in dramatic change. The answers sometimes give us positive reinforcement that we are in fact doing the right thing, and that the planning really is meeting the children's needs. In this case, no change is needed.

Feedback to parents – your child, your future

'Parents and/or carers should be kept up-to-date with their child's progress and development. Practitioners should address any learning and development needs in partnership with parents and/or carers, and any relevant professionals.'

Statutory Framework for the EYFS (DfE, 2012)

If we return to the triangular diagram presented earlier in the book, you will see that reporting features at the top of the triangle, where information is at its most condensed, where there is sometimes limited time or opportunity for feedback, and when the process can seem at its 'coldest' and most automatic. Of course this function of assessment (summative, annual meetings with parents and carers) does not represent the richness of contact with a child's parents during the early years, when the family is in closest touch with the setting and the adults who work there.

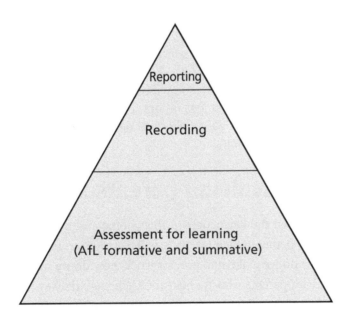

Reporting

Recording

Assessment for learning
(AfL formative and summative)

Giving feedback by reporting to parents and others is one of the most important aspects of assessment, because if we want the outcomes of our observations to be effective in improving learning and progress, everyone needs to know what is happening. Of course, it is much easier and more effective if the information, particularly at points of transition, is condensed and presented in a form that parents can understand.

However, this book is not just about summative assessment, its major focus is AfL, a process which is continuous throughout the year. If parents understand how this works, they can feel confident that they are helping their children in the best possible way.

In 2012, the government produced a leaflet for parents, explaining the changes to the EYFS and emphasising how important their role is. The section on assessment and reporting says:

> **'How can I find out how my child is getting on?**
> It is important that you and the professionals caring for your child work together. You need to feel comfortable about exchanging information and discussing things that will benefit your child. These conversations will either need to be with your childminder or, in a larger setting like a nursery, with your child's **"key person"**. This is the person who:
>
> - Is your main point of contact within the setting
> - Helps your child to become settled, happy and safe
> - Is responsible for your child's care, development and learning
> - Takes a careful note of your child's progress, sharing this with you and giving you ideas as to how to help your child at home
>
> You should be able to get information about your child's development at any time and there are two stages (at age 2, and again at age 5) when the professionals caring for your child must give you written information about how he or she is doing.'

Ten tips for involving parents in AfL

Children who know that the key people in their home and their Key Person in the setting are working together in their interests, will feel more secure, and will therefore learn better. So how do we make that process work, how do we make it manageable in a busy setting, with parents who are busy too? What are the key factors that work for good communication and inclusive practice in AfL in the early years? These **Ten** tips for involving parents in AfL may help, and they are all things you can easily build into regular practice in your setting:

1 **Recognise the parents' role as first educator, and start early** – make sure that parents' voices are heard before the child is admitted to your setting, visit them at home if you can, and explain what AfL looks like, bring some photos and include some of children talking with other adults or children about their work and parents spending time looking at folders or portfolios with their children. Find out what the child likes, dislikes, their interests and concerns. Make sure that the pre-admission visit is a positive experience, that you listen more than you talk, and that parents don't feel bombarded by questions that seem like a test! Make some notes and check them with the parents before you leave, so they know what you have written. This builds the sort of trust you need for real partnership.

    An example: *Pat and Sue, early years practitioners, visit a family together. One takes some toys, so they can play with the Tony (the child), the other talks with the parents and makes some notes. They have some prompts for their conversation, but these are not just questions, more invitations to tell them about the child. They take photo books of the setting in action, and an invitation to come for some pre-admission visits as a family. Before they leave, Pat (who will be the child's Key Person) asks if she may take a picture of the family together, explains a bit about her role and checks the notes with the parents before she leaves.*

2 **Make sure you use this early information** – it's no use if you just put it in a cupboard, so incorporate it in your planning for welcoming the child on the first steps in your setting. Make sure you have the sorts of things in your setting that will make the child feel secure. Spend time with them during the first days and weeks, as they show you what they can do. Feed back to parents on any inconsistencies in behaviour or any worries that you may have, but make sure these are presented positively!

    An example: *As Pat and Sue drive back to the setting, they talk about the family and how they can help Tony to settle. They note that he seems a rather lacking in confidence and may take longer to settle than some of the other children. They also note his interest in the photo book, and particularly the train track. This will be the first piece of information Pat puts in his Interest Tracker (a simple sheet in his portfolio that records his developing interests).*

3 **Include parents at every stage of the process** – if parents really feel they know you, and you are making a real effort for their child, they are almost certain to be more open to giving and getting information about their child. Remember that children only start school once, it's important to get it right, as we can't go back and do it again! First impressions are lasting ones for children and their parents.

An example: *This setting has a policy of staggered entry and pre-admission visits are spread over the last half term before the child enters. The children come in twos and threes, and visit while the previous group of children are still in the class. This seems to help in many ways.*

On Tony's pre-admission visit, there is a 'Welcome to Tony' poster on the door of the setting, with the photo of him with his family. The train set is out and some other boys welcome him by including him in their game. His mum and dad have both made the effort to come to this visit, and Pat makes sure she has time to talk to them, as she shows them round the setting, explaining what is going on. One of the older children is asked to show them her folder where she keeps originals, copies and photos of her learning, each one dated and some with comments written by the practitioners. There are also some comments from the girl's parents.

Before they leave, Pat gives the parents a card with her name and the contact numbers of the setting. On the back of the card are some simple tips for helping children to settle when they first start:

What you can do to help your child to settle in:
Read a story to them every day.
Make sure they have enough sleep.
Give them time to eat some breakfast, even if you don't.
Tell them you love them every day.
Tell us if you are going to be late at home time.

---

4 **Make your setting accessible** – go outside regularly and look at your front entrance with a parent's eyes. Does it look and feel welcoming? Do you have children's work or photos on display? Have you got helpful signs so they know where to go? Is there somewhere comfortable and welcoming to wait? Is there helpful information on parenting and the curriculum for parents on a notice board or table, and copies for them to take?

An example: *The entrance to this setting is very small, it is near a busy road. Obviously the staff must make sure the children are secure, but the practitioners have made the small area welcoming with flowers, a small settee, a basket of baby toys and a small notice board for information. There are also some photos of the setting in action. On the doors through to the three group rooms are photos of the children and adults who work there. On the outside of the door is a welcome notice in several languages.*

5 **Give plenty of informal opportunities for parents to contribute information** – *Do* parents genuinely feel welcome? Is there really an open door through which they can come, or do they get the message that you are very busy and they can only see you if they are very 'pushy' or have an emergency? Some parents find it very difficult to come into settings and although they may have some valuable information, they need encouragement to stay and talk.

An example: *Pat, Sue and their colleagues have worked hard to make the setting a place where parents can come at any time. They schedule their day so the children and their parents begin each session with child-initiated activities, which means the staff are available to listen to parents and to give them some informal feedback about how things are going. They can also explain what is happening when children play, by observing what is going on in the room.*

Photos of the setting at different times of the day are displayed, so parents see other activities where children are learning in groups, going to different parts of the building, meeting other adults or making new friends. There are also packs of sticky notes for parents to jot down significant information about home. Any important information about individual children, which everyone should share (such as new babies, holidays and so on), is written on a 'Breaking news' board, and the practitioners make a note of anything which is more confidential or sensitive.

6 **Include everyone** – some parents find it difficult to spend time in your setting because they are working, others are less confident, some have such stressful lives that they just can't face any more responsibility, and a very few remain stubbornly unavailable.

An example: *In Pat and Sue's setting, they make every effort to make sure every parent has equal access to information. They know the staff can't make parents use this, and there are some who don't. In addition to their availability at the start of each session, they encourage parents to choose the methods they find easiest. One parent, who is disabled, has weekly contact by phone to update information about her child's progress; another uses the Internet to email information – she knows she may not get a detailed reply, but it makes her feel much more involved. Some parents like diaries for messages from home – they know that the practitioners may not have time to reply every day, but they will always read and initial each entry, commenting if they feel the need. Others (particularly those whose children attend after-school care) ask for the children's profiles or some photos to keep them up to date (it is heartening to note that none of these vital collections has ever been lost!). The most recent development is a website blog from the setting, where parents can see photos and news from all the groups in the setting.*

7 **Meet regularly** – meet regularly to discuss the child, this is helpful, both in understanding the child and in building trust with parents. This *doesn't* mean frequent *formal* meetings, but making the most of the points in the day when parents are most likely to be around, and adding to these by offering other opportunities for parents to be involved in the life of the setting. For many parents, these opportunities will provide less threatening times and places for discussing their child. Of course you have to report formally every so often to discuss how their child is progressing against the curriculum objectives, but this conversation becomes a continuation of the relationship they are building with you, not a confrontation with the possibility of blame and guilt on their part. This is the sort of relationship that helps when you are bringing together information for the Two Year old Check and the Profile. In this way, you can easily incorporate information from parents, and parents never get a shock when they read the written report.

An example: *In Pat and Sue's setting the staff try to expand the opportunities for informal contact each year, and next year they are going to try offering an email service to working parents. This will build on the current 'incoming message system' by adding a feature where the children and staff can send emails to their parents, which, to begin with, will only be for photos of pieces of work or activities that will be included in the child's portfolio. If this works, they may expand it in the future but if it proves to be unmanageable, they may discontinue it.*

Existing opportunities to become involved include helping during sessions; accompanying the group on walks and visits; free access to their child's portfolio at the beginning and end of the day and an appointment system for longer discussions, particularly when parents are worried. They also meet with parents with their child every term to look together at the portfolio, and talk about next steps.

8 **Explain what you are doing** – if parents are to understand what you are trying to do in supporting AfL, they need you to explain and demonstrate what it is. Most parents will only have experienced more formal sorts of assessment, with marks and grades, with little explanation of how they could make their work better. If you do some specific things to support learning to learn, explain them to parents in photos, short notes home, newsletters and in meetings.

An example: *When Pat and Sue started to use AfL techniques, they had a workshop before they started to explain their plans to parents. This involved explaining what sharing learning intentions with children, and 'two stars and a wish' involved. Parents who couldn't attend the workshop could see what happened in photos displayed on the parents' notice board, and could take an explanatory sheet to read at home. The members of staff in the setting encourage parents to ask when they don't understand what is going on, as children do sometimes come home with a mixed description of what is happening!*

9 **Get the children to help** – the children will be enthusiastic about involving their parents. They love seeing their parents in their setting, and will welcome any opportunities to do this. Be imaginative, some parents find it difficult to come during the day – and this may make their children feel left out. How are you going to make opportunities for these parents to join their children? Remember that social events can make a big difference to working parents and those who are less confident, as they aren't too 'teachery'!

An example: *Pat, Sue and their colleagues have always welcomed parents into the setting, and they are always looking for new ways, of which the email system described above is one. Children are also encouraged to invite their parents to see what they have been doing during the day. They take photos home in their book bags, and they bring objects, photos and other significant objects to the setting, including an increasing range of the foods they eat and the clothes they wear at home, for festivals and special occasions. A small group of parents (including one dad) come in to cook with the children, widening the children's experiences of food from around the world.*

During last year they had a real push on involving dads, by helping the children to organise some Saturday gardening and DIY sessions to improve the outdoor environment – planting a sensory garden and building a new pond. The children wrote invitations and made posters, they also helped with the snacks, and really enjoyed helping their parents in the setting. Everyone loved these events and they were well supported, particularly the one with a barbecue at lunchtime, and more events are planned.

Many of these events are about enhancing experiences for children, but the great spin-off is a real community approach to education.

10 Don't be too ambitious – start small! – the setting described in the examples is very well established, the members of staff have worked in the setting for many years and know the area and the parents well. They have developed their work with parents over many years. Starting small is essential, decide on one thing you want to try next year, and don't expect one thing to fit all parents. Look carefully at the children and their families and decide on a suitable strategy that fits your unique setting and the unique families it supports. Ask a few parents what they would like to be more involved and informed about your work and how they can give you more information about their children. Try some of their ideas, and don't forget the children. Watch them, welcome their parents in and just get talking – this is often the very best way of getting going.

An example: when Pat and Sue started their work with parents, they thought they knew what the parents wanted. They drew up a rota for parent helpers and asked the parents to fill their names in for a regular slot. The parents in their area hated the idea! They were not organised enough to reserve a consistent commitment, and they were worried about what they would be asked to do. No-one signed up! Pat and Sue went back to the drawing board and considered some other ways that did not put so much pressure on the parents.

Parents have so much to offer us as we work with their children, but it is sometimes difficult to get the right balance between parental involvement and too much pressure on children, practitioners and parents themselves. However, in settings where parents feel really valued as their child's first and enduring teacher, the practitioners feel trusted and confident, children are happier, and happy children certainly learn more.

The next and final chapter in this book places the children firmly in focus as we conclude our journey through assessment for learning.

Involving the children – two stars and a wish for the future 9

Although this is the final chapter, it is far from just a conclusion! What you do with the information you collect from assessment, not merely to plan and track the curriculum, or compile annual reports to parents, but to change things for children, is one of the most important roles for you as a practitioner.

AfL in the early years

The previous chapter addressed how you could use AfL to inform your planning for future learning. This chapter is about using the same information to help children and their families to understand what they are learning now and how to improve learning in the future.

Of course, older children can be helped to do this by displaying posters, written comments, helpful marking, talk partners, traffic lights, 'no hands up' and all the other well-publicised AfL techniques that encourage children to think about learning.

In the early years it is both more difficult and more important to harness the power of feedback. Very young children live for the moment, and need immediate feedback, and they respond more to pictures than words, and more to people than to paper, however brightly coloured the poster might be! They need their feedback to be tailored to their current interests and to be worded in ways that support their confidence and competence as young learners. If we give them too much information, or messages that are too complex, we risk undermining their self-image and self-esteem. Instead of becoming more competent and confident, some may shut down and become passive, over-reliant on adults, or even worse, aggressively defensive.

However, the majority of young children are smart and resilient! They know when we are being honest with them, and they have a very good idea of how much effort they have been making. They may need some help in identifying what 'good' means in any given situation, but once they do, they can become very reflective about their own and others' learning:

'All children have a right to be listened to and valued in the setting. Children enjoy and can become very able at thinking about and assessing their own learning and development if this is recognised and supported well. They can help to record their progress, and identify what they have enjoyed or found difficult. Very young children, and those with speech or other developmental delay or disability may not say anything or very little verbally, but they will communicate a great deal in other ways. This might be through gesture, action, body language and signing.'

Know How, The Progress check at age two (NCB; 2012)

To be successful, feedback for young children should always be:

- honest
- specific to the child, their interests and abilities
- positively worded
- balanced
- relevant to them
- timely, and close to the action
- focused on the learning, not on the child
- frequent, but not constant.

Feedback can backfire or become counter-productive, particularly for very young children, if it is:

- **too kind** – '*What a clever girl, you* **have** *worked hard!*'
- **too vague** – '*That's lovely!*'
- **too critical** – '*That's wrong!*
- **too excessive** – '*What a wonderful painting you have done, you're a real artist!*'
- **too late** – '*I just want to say that I think you were a really kind friend when we went to the park last week*'.

Examples added to quote from *Assessment for Learning: A Practical Guide* (CCEA, 2009).

Keeping the balance of positive reinforcement and honest support for improvement is important, and the techniques for using AfL need practice, particularly when working with very young children, where we sometimes have less room for manoeuvre or time for reflection. Fortunately, the people who are constructing today's early years guidance have taken note of research, and are incorporating key elements into the curriculum that are not only helpful to brain development and delivery of the curriculum, but in AFL.

In the UK, the Northern Ireland Council for Curriculum, Examinations and Assessment (CCEA) has been in the forefront of embedding AfL in the National Curriculum, making it more than a way of simply monitoring progress, but the key way to improve learning. This work has resulted in *Assessment for Learning: A Practical Guide*, which gives guidance to teachers in Northern Ireland, and has been a significant influence on the latest version of the curriculum for the early years (The Foundation Stage), where guidance helpfully describes AfL in the early years in these ways:

> 'Effective questioning is also an integral part of observation and assessment practice in the Foundation Stage.
>
> - Adults should use *questioning* to:
> - clarify or extend children's thinking;
> - interact sensitively with children to support their learning on topics of mutual interest;
> - engage children in reflective discussion about their learning;
> - make judgements on what children understand and can do;
> - model the effective use of questioning.
>
> *Feedback in the Foundation stage should primarily be oral and should take place throughout the learning process.* When giving feedback to children, adults should remember:
>
> - young children need a nurturing climate;
> - verbal and non-verbal language from the adult gives powerful messages to the child about his/her ability;
> - to focus feedback on individual progress;
> - to give feedback that focuses on success and improvement; and
> - to give children time to make improvements.'
>
> *Understanding the Foundation Stage* (CCEA, 2006).

The learning environment

For such guidance to be effective practitioners should be aware of the learning environment on young children, and here *Assessment for Learning: A Practical Guide* can help us. The three essentials are **structure, skills and information.** After each of the these (below), I have explored what each one means for early years practitioners trying to establish AfL for children under five:

> '*Structure*: Classrooms with significant levels of independent learning tend to be much more structured. They have clear procedures for everything, from accessing and returning resources and pursuing learning activities, to using the teacher's feedback to make improvements in learning.'

High quality curriculum guidance for the early years across the world promotes independent learning, supporting practitioners in providing child-led activities in 'Enabling environments'. Independent learning can only flourish in an environment where some things are predictable, and there is an order and permanence to the day, to objects and to relationships.

> '*Skills*: Invest time in helping pupils to develop their independent learning skills. Teach them how to ask and answer questions, how to use success criteria to negotiate learning activities and use feedback effectively, and how to manage the demanding skills of reflecting about their own (and others') learning.'

Early years settings are places where children have the opportunity to both learn and practise key skills. An essential part of developing skills is to have good models! Young children need time to develop skills, they need to see adults and older children modeling learning and personal skills in ways that inspire young learners to learn them too. Being an independent thinker, a good questioner and a reflective practitioner are essentials for those working in the early years.

> '*Information*: Provide sets of information in child-friendly language that enable pupils to access support during their learning activities. This information may be in the form of success criteria or reminders of strategies and procedures, such as questioning and feedback. These play an important role in reducing the pressure on pupils' memory to hold such information. This can often make the difference between independence and over-reliance on you or their peers.'

Of course, most of the children in the early years are just beginning to become readers and writers, so 'child-friendly language' will need to be mainly spoken, with pictorial clues to help young memories. Pictures, words and simple language will be most effective in the early years setting, but this does not mean patronising children or lowering our expectations. As most of us know, children are much smarter than we might think, and can take much more control of their own learning than we sometimes allow.

Once they are able to read simple text, these expectations could be presented in the following format, with pictures and words:

Learning intention	Success criteria
We are learning to help at clearing up time. 	• Remember where things are kept. • Help with everything, not just the things you have been playing with. • Everyone helps.
We are learning to listen to each other. 	• Look at the person who is speaking. • Don't do anything else while they are speaking. • Think about what they are saying.

In early years settings, the setting and evaluating of group expectations is likely to be a weekly occurrence, with intentions frequently focusing on big learning issues, such as 'working together' and 'good listening'.

A checklist for linking The Characterisitcs of Effective Learning in the EYFS with Assessment for Learning?

If we construct an 'AfL in the early years checklist', what will it contain, and what are the challenges it will present to us? How can we use the Characteristics of Effective Learning in the EYFS to help with assessment for learning?

1 *Independent learning* – **settings where independent learning is embedded appear to offer children a magical balance of freedom, clear structures for learning, and safe risk, which results in better learning.**
    What does independent learning look like in our setting? Is it true independence (autonomy) or are children just engaged in 'hands on, brains off' play activities with no structure and no support from us, while we do something else? Are children able to take 'safe risks', both in the environment and in their learning? Do we subtly make choices for children by 'putting things out' for them, or suggesting that some activities are more important to us than others? The Characteristics of Effective Learning give some help, particularly in Creating and Thinking Critically, where the advice includes:

    'In planning activities, ask yourself: Is this an opportunity for children to find their own ways to represent and develop their own ideas? Avoid children just reproducing someone else's ideas.'
    'Development Matters, Characteristics of Effective Learning, Creating and Thinking Critically (Early Education; 2012)

2 *Clear learning intentions* – **settings where practitioners share clear learning intentions with children are more likely to be able to implement AfL. If children are clear about what we expect them to learn, they are much more likely to be able to concentrate on the activity and talk about whether they are successful.**
    Do we present independent learning in a framework of clear expectations?

How do children know what we want them to learn? How do we share learning intentions with them? How often do we discuss these when the activity is over?

'Give feedback and help children to review their own progress and learning. Talk with children about what they are doing, how they plan to do it, what worked well and what they would change next time.'
Development Matters, Characteristics of Effective Learning, Creating and Thinking Critically (Early Education; 2012)

3 *A focus on children as individuals* – **settings where practitioners know about individuals and their families, observing children to find out their current interests and any difficulties will be able to support AfL. The Key Person approach supports AfL. If children understand that adults know them as individuals, appreciate their strengths, interests, worries and fears, they will be more confident as they learn how to learn and evaluate their own learning.**
Do we really know each child as an individual? How do children know that we are interested in them as individuals? How do we include their families, cultures and interests as we plan new experiences?

'Help children to become aware of their own goals, make plans, and to review their own progress and successes. Describe what you see them trying to do, and encourage children to talk about their own processes and successes.'
Development Matters, Characteristics of Effective Learning, Active Learning (Early Education; 2012)

4 *Sensitive questioning* – **settings where practitioners are good at asking open questions that really make children think will be nurturing AfL. These practitioners will also be good at encouraging children to ask questions as well as answering them!**
Do we know how to ask open questions? Do children have opportunities to ask questions too? How much time do we give to 'sustained shared thinking' where adults and children spend time thinking together?

'Value questions, talk, and many possible responses, without rushing toward answers too quickly.'
Development Matters, Characteristics of Effective Learning, Creating and Thinking Critically (Early Education; 2012)

5 *Prompts and reminders of our expectations* – **settings where practitioners help children to get it right by reminding them appropriately about what is expected of them, and by modelling thinking, questioning, trying things out, even making mistakes, so children know that is the way to become a good learner.**

Are we clear about what we expect? Do we remind children, before and during activities of what we are expecting (our criteria for success)? Are we good models for the children in our care – do we practice what we preach? Do we make our expectations for the whole group explicit, and do we praise children when they reach them?

'Model being a thinker, showing that you don't always know, are curious and sometimes puzzled, and can think and find out.'
Development Matters, Characteristics of Effective Learning, Creating and Thinking Critically (Early Education; 2012)

6 *Keeping feedback positive* – **settings where positive feedback outnumbers suggestions for improvement, and negative feedback is phrased in positive terms, are more likely to be successful. There is evidence that the ratio of two to one, two positives to each point for improvement is the best balance for maintaining a positive environment and relationships. This is sometimes referred to as 'two stars and a wish', where children are more likely to be able to focus on improvement, while still feeling successful.**

Do we keep this ideal balance when giving feedback to children? Do children get two stars and a wish from us, and are they clear about which is which? Do we model this when we feed back to each other as practitioners?

'Give feedback and help children to review their own progress and learning.'
Development Matters, Characteristics of Effective Learning, Creating and Thinking Critically (Early Education; 2012)

7 *A focus on clear feedback and next steps* – **children in settings where they have clear feedback will be more confident and more likely to become better learners. If they also have some idea of where to go next (the ways they could improve)**

Is our feedback to children really clear, and focused on the learning intentions and criteria for success? Do we really help children to understand what they can do to improve, and is this clearly linked to the learning intentions we have shared with them?

'Talk with children about what they are doing, how they plan to do it, what worked well and what they would change next time.'
Development Matters, Characteristics of Effective Learning, Creating and Thinking Critically (Early Education; 2012)

8 *Making it manageable* – managing this process is time consuming and can result in pressure for practitioners and children. Deep concentrated feedback is not possible for every child in every activity every day. The ideal times are during child-initiated learning, when you may have more time to get involved in asking children what they plan to do, and in detailed discussions of outcomes; or at the end of an adult-led, small group activity, where the learning intention is clear and the session is short enough for children to remember!

How are we managing feedback so it does not become a pressure on us or on the children? Do we sometimes ask children what they are intending to do during child-initiated activities? Do we follow this up with conversations about how successful they are in reaching their own goals? Do we make our intentions clear for adult-led activities, so children know clearly when they have achieved them?

'Play is a key opportunity for children to think creatively and flexibly, solve problems and link ideas. Establish the enabling conditions for rich play: space, time, flexible resources, choice, control, warm and supportive relationships.'
Development Matters, Characteristics of Effective Learning, Creating and Thinking Critically (Early Education; 2012)

Examples of the process in action

One of the most useful ways to understand AfL in the early years is through examples of the process in action, in visits to settings where practitioners are trying the methods; by listening to or reading about practitioners as they talk or write about what they do; or by reading case studies and snippets of practice. Of course these can only give glimpses into the lives of children in our settings, but may help confirm what we know should be happening as we support children in thinking about learning.

Here are some examples:

> ***Trisha is playing with Garry***, *a baby who is just learning to walk unaided. She holds his hands and says 'Let's try that again – that's right, move one foot at a time. Can you let go of my hand? Good balancing!'*

Although Garry may not be able to understand everything Trisha is saying, but he knows she is concentrating on him and she is clear about what she is giving praise for, not just saying 'Good boy'.

> ***Neil brings his wobbly 'junk' model of a truck to show Sara***, *and as he reaches her two wheels fall off. Sara helps him to pick them up, saying, 'You said you were going to make a model today, and you have. It looks very interesting, tell me about it.' ''s a truck like my dad's' says Neil. 'Your dad sometimes lets you sit in his truck, doesn't he?' Neil nods. 'How did you make it?' 'Boxes and glue' says Neil. 'What happened to the wheels?' 'Falled off.' 'How could you fix them better, so they don't fall of when you take it home?' 'More tape.' 'Let's go to the making table and see if we can find some, then maybe you'd like to take a photo?'*

Sara confirms what Neil said his intentions were, gives plenty of praise, a suggestion that he could improve the truck, and a way of recording what he has done, so he can take his model home.

> ***Four girls are playing in the outside area***. *They are making a den with some fabric and canes, but they are having problems making the den stay up so they can play inside. They see Colleen (a practitioner) and ask her to help. They want her to fix the den for them, but she has different ideas! 'Can you fix this den?' the girls ask. 'What are you trying to do? If you explain, I can help you to do it' says Colleen, 'What do you think you need?' The girls explain what they want to do.*
>
> *'We need some clips to fix the material' says one girl. 'Do you know where to find them?' says Colleen. 'I do' says another girl. The two go off to search and soon come back with some pegs. 'We found some string too' they say. Building continues, with Colleen playing her part as a member of the group, leaving when the structure is stable and the girls can use it for their play. Later, she asks the girls to tell her how the game went. The girls are enthusiastic about their den and their intentions to return to it tomorrow to make improvements and decorate the outside.*

Colleen acts as a member of the group, modelling problem solving, not giving the answers. She does not solve their problems for them, asking open questions and gently pushing the solving of the problems back to the children. She stays with the group as they work on the structure, but leaves when she is no longer needed. She remembers to ask the girls to bring her up to date later and suggests they should tell the rest of the group how they made their den.

> **Two boys begin to shout and argue** over the red bike in the pre-school. All the children think the red bike is the 'best bike', and there is always a rush to grab it at the beginning of the session. Nadia goes over to intervene, 'What is happening?' she says. 'I got it first!'. 'No, I got it first!' say the two boys, continuing to pull at the red bike. 'Please put the bike down while we talk about it' says Nadia, and the boys reluctantly let go.
>
> 'I know you both want the bike, what can we do about that?' says Nadia. Both children are still very upset and neither speaks. 'Well, what did we say yesterday when Jay and Jamie both wanted the bike?' 'Share it' says one. 'Yes, share it, and how did we agree to do that?' 'With the timer.' 'Yes, so do you want to get the timer and then we'll decide who is going first.'
>
> The children go happily together and return with the sand timer. Nadia holds it behind her back (as agreed with the whole group) and the children guess which hand it is in. The boy who is right gets on the bike, while the other sits with Nadia, holding the timer. Nadia says to them 'You worked that out really well. What will you do next time you both want the bike?'

This situation is very common in early years settings where there is always the 'best bike' or an equivalent popular toy. The difference in this setting is that the practitioners helped the children to solve the problem and come up with a solution, which is now an expectation. Nadia knows that it takes time for children to get used to new arrangements, they are impetuous and need support to get things right. She praises them for remembering the new arrangement and reinforces what they should do next time.

> **Jamal is in his third term in Reception**. He has been experimenting with mixing his own paint for a pattern-making activity. He brings his painting to show his teacher, Jan. She sits at a table and looks at the painting with Jamal.
>
> 'Well done', she says, 'you have made lots of colours by mixing the

paints, how did you make the pattern?' Jamal smiles and points to the top of the paper 'I started the pattern here', he says, 'It's all squares and the colours go in turns.' 'I can see that', says Jan, tracing some of the squares with her finger, and saying the names of the colours. 'Was it a hard thing to do? How did you remember the pattern?' 'Yes, I kept forgetting the next colour!' says Jamal, 'but then I got it in my head and remembered it in my brain, it's brown, blue, red, green, brown, blue, red, green, and I kept saying it.' 'Good thinking, and good remembering.' Says Jan. 'I think we should take a photo and I'll write down how you remembered the pattern.' 'And put it in my red folder, and then I'm going to do another one – I know how to do it now, and this one will be much better!' says Jamal.

Careful, open questions, positively put, enable Jan to find out whether Jamal understands what the task was and whether he has achieved it. He is beginning to think about *how* he remembers things, and is feeling very successful. He is also able to set his own targets for improvement as he works on the second pattern.

***The children in Acorn group** are just embarking on a centre of interest about their local park, which they visit regularly throughout the year. They have just returned from an autumn walk with their pockets full of acorns and other things they have found. Lisa is working with them to think about what they have experienced and what they want to find out about. She sits with the children on the carpet, with a big piece of paper and some big felt-tipped pens, and reminds the children about what they were looking for today at the park. The children say 'autumn things', 'seeds', 'leaves', 'sticks'.*

Lisa draws a picture of the park gates in the middle of the paper and begins to talk with the children about what they saw, heard, smelled, touched and even tasted at the park, framing their thoughts by using their senses. They start with things they saw. As they work on the mind map together, the children select from their collections and place them on the paper. Some children draw pictures of the things they saw or heard that they couldn't collect. Lisa prompts them to remember where they went and some of the things they heard or touched. They pass round the camera and look at the pictures they took, to remind themselves of what they chose to photograph.

Lisa also uses questions to encourage the children to think – 'What did we see at the other side of the pond?' 'Where did the dog go when he ran away? Who do you think he belongs to?' and 'Where is that thing you found Paul – that thing we didn't know the name of?' 'Can you remember what we wanted to find out about ducks?' 'We found some green tree seeds like wings, who brought those? How can we find out what they are?' 'What was that smell we smelled by the gate – the smell that made us all feel hungry?'

Lisa is skilfully scaffolding the children's learning as she takes them back through the walk in the park, reminding them of all the experiences they had, and helping them to shape them into some lines of enquiry for future learning, and further things to look for on their next visit. She will photograph the 3D mind map and use it as a centrepiece for a display that will grow during the next days and weeks as children find out more about autumn in their park. Their activities will involve painting, making collages and arrangements of the objects, bringing more findings to nursery, watching the weather, using simple reference books and telling stories about their own local park keeper who comes to visit and read *Percy the Park Keeper* with them.

I conclude this book here, firmly with the children, who are at the heart of the process of learning, supported there by practitioners who are interested in them, not just as empty vessels to be filled and then measured, but as individuals, each one capable of thinking for themselves.

Children have a right to be in control of their own learning, we can't get inside their heads, but we can create a climate conducive to them doing it themselves, and I can think of no better way of expressing this than in the following quote. It is taken from Pre-birth to Three, Scotland's Guidance on good practice in the early years, and encapsulates the principles in this book:

> 'Babies and young children are individuals, each with their own unique talents and abilities. Effective staff within early years settings seek to ensure that learning experiences, routines and activities build on information provided by parents and start with children's needs and interests. Planning begins with skilful and purposeful observation of children, and this enables staff to draw conclusions and plan next steps.
>
> Assessing children in terms of their progress and needs is an ongoing process and is integral to planning, observation and implementation. By using this information effectively, staff, parents and children, where appropriate, can create and maintain plans which help to provide a focused and individualised approach.'
>
> *Pre-Birth to Three; Positive outcomes for children and families*
> *(Learning and Teaching Scotland, 2010)*

Guy Claxton's *Building Learning Power* (2002) deals with the practical application of his ideas. In it he introduces us to four new 'Rs' that he would like to see replace the three traditional ones when thinking about what learning power consists of:

> '**Resilience**: "being ready, willing and able to lock on to learning". Being able to stick with difficulty and cope with feelings such as fear and frustration.
>
> **Resourcefulness**: "being ready, willing and able to learn in different ways". Having a variety of learning strategies and knowing when to use them.
>
> **Reflection**: "being ready, willing and able to become more strategic about learning". Getting to know our own strengths and weaknesses.
>
> **Relationships**: "being ready, willing and able to learn alone and with others".'

These features, often apparent when children are involved in play which they have initiated themselves, can lead to a state sometimes referred to as 'flow'.

Mihaly Csikszentmihalyi (a Hungarian psychology professor, now working in the USA) describes '**flow**' as –

> '...a state of concentration or complete absorption with the activity at hand and the situation. It is a state in which people are so involved in an activity that nothing else seems to matter. The idea of flow is identical to the feeling of being *in the zone* or *in the groove*. The flow state is an optimal state of intrinsic motivation, where the person is fully immersed in what they are doing. This is a feeling everyone has at times, characterized by a feeling of great absorption, engagement, fulfilment, and skill—and during which temporal concerns (time, food, ego-self, etc.) are typically ignored.'

If we offer children opportunities to experience 'flow' in our schools and settings (and we should), we must also join them in their play, to observe and celebrate deep learning, where the children in our care show us what they really can do!

Bibliography and Further Reading

Active Learning Methods for Key Stage 1 and 2; Northern Ireland; Council for the Curriculum, Examinations and Assessment (CCEA); 2007

Assessment and Reporting Arrangements 2013 (ARA); Standards and Testing Agency; 2012

Assessment and Reporting Arrangements 2013: Foundation Stage (ARA); Standards and Testing Agency; 2012

Assessment for Learning: A Practical Guide; The Council for the Curriculum, Examinations and Assessment (Northern Ireland); 2009

Conception to age 2 – the age of opportunity, Addendum to the Government's vision for the Foundation Years: Supporting Families in the Foundation Years, Wave Trust/DFE, 2013

Curriculum for Excellence, Building the Curriculum 5: A Framework for Assessment; The Scottish Government; 2010

Development Matters in the Early Years Foundation Stage; Early Education; 2012

Early Years Education: An International Perspective; Tony Bertram and Chris Pascal; Centre for Research in Early Childhood, Birmingham UK; 2002

Early Years Foundation Stage Parents Guide to the Framework; DFE; 2012

Early Years Foundation Stage Profile Handbook; Standards and Testing Agency; 2012

Early Years Foundation Stage Profile exemplification materials – from WEB

Education (Pupil Information) (England) Regulations; 2005; www.legislation.gov.uk

Educating Young Children: Active Learning Processes for Preschool and Childcare Programs; Hohmann, Mary and Weikart, David P.; High/Scope Publications; 2002

Effective practice: Observation, Assessment and Planning; *The Early Years Foundation Stage* CD-ROM; Department for Children, Schools and Families (England); 2008

Foundation Phase Child Development Profile Guidance; Department for Children, Education, Lifelong Learning and Skills (Wales); 2009

Framework for Children's Learning for 3-7 Year Olds in Wales; Department for Children, Education and Lifelong Learning and Skills; 2008

Inside the Black Box: Raising Standards Through Classroom Assessment; Paul Black and Dylan William; King's College London School of Education; 2001

Know How Guide to Two Year old Assessment; National Children's Bureau, 2012

Learning, Playing and Interacting: Good Practice in the Early Years Foundation Stage; Department for Children, Schools and Families (England); 2009

Observing Children; Department for Children, Education, Lifelong Learning and Skills (Wales); 2008

Pre-Birth to Three – Positive Outcomes for Scotland's Children and Families, Learning and Teaching Scotland; 2010

Reporting pupils' progress to parents in the Early Years; Ofqual; 2011

Statutory assessment arrangements for the end of Foundation Phase and Key Stages 2 and 3, Welsh Government; 2013

Statutory Framework for the Early Years Foundation Stage; DFE, 2012

Supporting Families in the Foundation Years, Department for Education/Department of Health, 2013

Te Whariki, Early Childhood Curriculum; Ministry of Education (New Zealand); 1996

The Nature and Value of Formative Assessment for Learning; Paul Black; King's College London School of Education; 2004

Understanding the Foundation Stage; Early Years Inter-board publication: The Council for the Curriculum, Examinations and Assessment (Northern Ireland); 2006

Unlocking Formative Assessment, Practical Strategies for Enhancing Pupils' Learning in the Primary Classroom; Clarke, Shirley; Hodder Education; 2001